The
Pure, Golden
Light of Love

A scientist's new and startling
report on the discovery of
God's Great Plan for life on Earth

H. King

SPIRIT
HOUSE
PRESS

P.O. Box 37163
Tucson, AZ 85740-7163

This special edition was prepared for printing by Ghost River Images, 1600 East Roger Road #22, Tucson, Arizona 85719.

This book is printed on special acid-free paper
for maximum life.

Printed in the United States of America

First Printing: 1993

10 9 8 7 6 5 4 3 2 1

Library of Congress catalog number 93-84329
ISBN 0-9636849-2-2

DIRECTORY

This page is left blank for your own directory.

TABLE OF CONTENTS

Part I
Physical and Spiritual Journeys (1968-1988)

Part II
Dialogues with an Ascended Master (1988-1993)

A FEW WORDS
TO THE SCIENCE COMMUNITY

The events and thought transmissions described in these pages do not and cannot provide the hard, verifiable proofs currently demanded by the scientific method. However, I have come as close to such proof as I could, presenting occurences as accurately and precisely as possible, taking notes and statements as they unfolded.

Of course, this isn't "scientific proof" which requires others to repeat the experiment and obtain similar results. In two instances, my assistant at work, a trained chemist, described to me events which he experienced (his being "overshadowed" as mentioned in the Christian Bible), once while he was in my presence, and once while alone. But how to PROVE this to others? Some have said "How about miracles?" Still, even witnessing such an event isn't proof to those not there, and sometimes not even to those who are. Many books have been written stating that the so-called "miracles" of Christ weren't miracles at all; just common events which the participants mistook or exaggerated. For instance in St. Matthew (Chapter 14, 14-21), when Christ fed a great multitude (about 5000) with just five loaves and two fishes, it has been suggested that there was no actual creation of more food, just that many attendees who had food with them shared it with others.

So how to PROVE the statements in this book? If you were an investigator of the non-material, where others can't "see," "hear," "record," or "measure" what you are "told," is there any solution? Yes, if you are willing to dedicate the years that I have, and experience for yourself what I have reported here. If you did, would you have precisely the same results? Your results would necessarily be somewhat different from mine because YOU are different from me. We are dealing here

1

with uniquely INDIVIDUAL abilities, rates of growth, understanding, and expressions, which are partly based on one's culture, education and reasoning faculties. However, your overall experience should remain essentially the same.

The amount of data and thought transmissions presented here are massive. I have presented them in the sequence that they occurred, and specified exactly when they occurred, so you can follow my steps as closely as possible. Occasionally I have added a later input to a specific event, to help you (and usually me as well) understand why an event may have happened as it did. But who is actually writing this book? As this story progressed, and my knowledge and capability to understand evolved, I gradually changed, developing new and different characteristics.

Because of these qualifications, please read this book with as open a mind as possible. How would you have reacted if similar, precise information and statements had suddenly been presented to you after many years of study and effort? You would probably have been as startled and as doubtful as I was, even after searching so diligently. Try to become "the disinterested observer" I tried to be—watching, listening, trying to record and understand what I "knew" was stated in my mind. Resist being too analytical too soon. Wait until you complete this book and follow the directions in order to actively feel some of the energies I was startled to encounter before you declare all this "nonsense".

Much of this information discusses YOUR future. As you read these words, you will discover that they are often more reasonable and sensible, based on our present level of science, than many previous concepts or theories. It is vital that you learn as much as you can from this book, and follow its suggestions as well as you are able, if you and others now on Earth wish to survive the coming Great Transition!

INTRODUCTION

This is the true story of one of the most remarkable and successful journeys of recent times. A journey that has been underway for 25 years and which is expected to continue for many more. It is the story of a quest to conquer time, space, and knowledge, using just the powers of the mind and soul. Of learning how to follow in the steps of previous explorers of the unknown who sought to become one with the Eternal Light. During this journey answers to universal questions were discovered: What is God? What is Life? Why are we here? Is spiritual growth possible? Startlingly, clear and unambiguous answers were found to these and many other questions.

But this isn't the story of only one individual. This journey is built on the thousands of years of struggle by countless others. Each new seeker is responsible to help others to either begin or further their own quest for fulfillment. This responsibility is the reason for this book.

The Pure, Golden Light of Love is about the experiences of light and love, enlightenment and empowerment, wisdom and wonder. Enjoy it. Learn from it. Discover your own path to understanding. Realize your unique heritage to become one with the Light.

Can all this new information and the startling experiences described here really be true? The only proof must utilize your own inner experience. Practice and discover truth yourself! Become your own exploratory scientist. In these pages you will find answers to questions that you have wondered about all your life. If you follow the directions for growth given here you will begin to understand, and then gain new insight into, this physical world as well as the world of the unknown. But YOU must make an effort to gain this new knowledge. Don't expect to grow by letting someone else do all the work for you. You must ACTIVELY desire to discover knowledge and wisdom if you wish to progress into what is usually called the unknown, making it at least partially knowable. The help and guidance you need to begin, and then deepen, your journey are contained in these pages. The choice is yours whether to gain in understanding and learn how to help yourself and others, or to remain in ignorance about your true capabilities.

The Beginning

I had reached my fortieth birthday before I knew that the world of the unknown might really exist! After almost 20 years of being a "proper" and boring chemical engineer and research scientist, I "happened" to pick up a book on yoga philosophy my wife had left on the dining room table. What a revelation! Did there really exist knowledge and ideas "out there" that scientists didn't know about? Information they had no interest in investigating with their usual care and thoroughness? Perhaps they just didn't know HOW or WHERE to begin? Maybe some felt that their peers would frown on them if they started to tinker with, and write about, information that might be essentially impossible to prove. Others may have thought (as I did until I really began studying it) that this is all nonsense.

We're all familiar with the old proverb, "Fools rush in where wise men fear to tread." Meet one such fool! Can you imagine anyone spending more than twenty years of the most intensive effort and study just to finally reach a point where they begin to feel "somewhat comfortable" with this strange wonderland of ancient (and now modern) knowledge and wisdom? Little did I know when I first began this journey how long it would take and to where it would lead.

At age forty, then, I began a more than twenty year period, aimed specifically at learning more about "the unknown," or "the world of the spirit". The words "God," "death, and "life" took on totally new meanings. This new project demanded the study of hundreds of books, travel to almost every sacred place on Earth (some more than once), and work with shamans in both the United States and the jungles, mountains and plains of Peru. It especially demanded meditation, meditation, and more meditation, as I first tried to understand, then finally, began to more fully utilize this very strange machine we call the brain.

This journey into the unknown proved to be the most difficult I have ever undertaken because in the unknown there are no proven rules, or even guidelines to follow and, initially at least, no "Master" to teach you. Only curiosity and the demand for more knowledge pulled me forward, with no way to verify whether the books I read are true, someone's wild imagination, or some of each. And, what to think when I suddenly started "knowing" or "hearing" information or thoughts that I had never read or heard before.

This book details this wondrous quest—which continues to this day. In it you will visit many of the most spiritual places on Earth. You will follow me step-by-step, as words begin to appear "out of nowhere" in my mind. You will learn how to actually feel and experience energies which begin to surround you as you plunge forward with me, going where few have ever gone before. To literally experience many of the energies discovered during this journey, simply sit back and relax. Then reread the description of a particular energy transfer. Now close your eyes and using YOUR IMAGINATION (this part is critical to your success), begin to FEEL these energies flowing through you. Finally sit quietly for a few minutes and allow these energies to actually generate themselves and to flow within you. You may have to practice this several times, but soon you should be able to really experience at least some of the truths I experienced.

In this book you will learn about—and begin to understand—both the near and distant future of our race, and of the planet Earth. You will learn that your unique "cell" was brought to Earth and how you evolved from that. You will learn how to use your psychic energy to heal others (if you wish to, and if your present body is capable of directing and controlling the necessary energies). You will learn about REAL space and time travel, not those in the imaginations of science fiction writers.

You are invited to participate in, and feel the awe of, each new discovery and happening. The wonders described here transcend the imagination. All these experiences actually happened, and were carefully recorded as I was led, one step at a time, along this most strange and mysterious path to truth and wisdom. Join me as I relive this unbelievable twenty-five year journey into the unknown. However, be aware that some of the statements "received" are very strange, and hard to believe. I make no claim WHEN some of the predictions will occur. I only know that I have, as accurately and clearly as possible, repeated exactly what was discovered.

This book is unlike any you have ever read, because its function is not to entertain you or just give you information. Its primary function is to act as a guide to the next species of humans as they are created, begin to multiply, and then assume control of the Earth. This guide is also meant to help humanity clearly understand the mistakes made by the races currently populating the Earth. It is to guide members of both the new species, and the current species of mankind, in what must be done, as well as what must NOT be done, to regenerate the Earth and build a new and vastly superior civilization.

This book is intended to act as a guide to humanity for the next one to two thousand years, offering knowledge, wisdom, and understanding. It describes how the author was brought into consciousness and what he was taught during this epic journey. These clear, simple teachings, while primarily given for the new species, can be very useful to those now on Earth if they wish to help prepare the Earth for the Great Transition— which is about to occur.

These teachings, acquired through direct mind-to-mind contact, are much more precise and exact than any that could be acquired by individual voice contact, or through the written word. Voice communications are fraught with disadvantages. One often struggles to find the right word to convey a particular idea or to try to give some information, while attempting to withhold or perhaps modify, other information. With such problems in just one language, imagine the difficulties involved trying to communicate in a language other than your "mother tongue," or from one culture to another. Often we think that we fully understand a statement or a translation, without realizing that totally different ideas may be involved. Consider the difference between two translations of the SAME book.

A similar problem is involved in trying to use the teachings of our present bibles, which were intended to give guidance to individuals and cultures under totally different circumstances, in totally different time periods, AND in different languages. These texts are often the result of translations from two or three different languages AND cultures, while trying to combine statements made in two or more time periods into a much later one. (Think about how our language and culture has changed in just the last one to two hundred years!)

Furthermore, translators often had to decide which statements to keep and which to discard, and then, in what order to present them. Often original ideas were either totally lost, or so changed that they may now do more harm than good. For instance, the idea that present life is sacred and should be preserved at all cost. This may have been fine as a general guideline when there wasn't the technology to literally "cheat death." But today, when the Earth is already vastly overpopulated and life can be maintained almost indefinitely, how ridiculous and childlike!

This book—and the ones to follow—are, therefore, attempts to begin anew, and to make available new and much clearer information about this planet, its support systems, and the PURPOSE of all life. This new information is to help begin the healing processes vitally needed to repair the terrible damage done to Pacha Mama (our Earth) over the last few hundred years.

As we travel this wonderful voyage of discovery together, remember that these words are written to act as guides both for those now on Earth and for future generations, after Earth's Great Transition. But it is especially offered to those of the new species now being created from our seed by The Watchers (The Spiritual Hierarchy). Their path will be full of difficulties and pitfalls. Hopefully just to know that others have already stumbled down this path, and left an occasional road sign for them, will ease their pain and allow them to more fully enjoy the wonders they are about to behold!

PART I
PHYSICAL & SPIRITUAL JOURNEYS
(1968—1988)

The Pure, Golden Light of Love

CHAPTER 1

THE QUEST BEGINS

Reading my wife's book on yoga marked the beginning of my quest. But now, how to begin the search for knowledge that might be out there? I went first to a local bookstore where I purchased 7 books on various forms of yoga. The word "yoga" means "yoke" in Sanskrit, and its study is intended to help an individual link physical and spiritual abilities into one. A few books proved interesting, but most weren't worth bothering with. Even getting started was proving more difficult than expected because I couldn't find a straightforward, college-style text that included what I thought I needed. Each author seemed to have totally different ideas and few seemed interested in PROVING the knowledge and wisdom that they discussed by testing it on themselves.

After digesting all of these books, a trip to a different book store yielded more of the same—a few fair books and many that were awful—at least for what I thought I was looking for. However, I was beginning to learn enough to realize that the first step in this investigation had to be meditation (or looking within) and more reading—always more searching and reading.

One of the biggest problems was turning out to be that none of these authors wrote in plain English. You would read hundreds of words but when you tried to state what you had just learned that might be useful, it proved to be little or nothing. I was used to reading scientific books and articles where the author first clearly states the problem to be investigated, usually along with past history. He or she then specifies and defines the tools to be used and the proposed effort. The test method is then described followed by test results. Finally the author gives conclusions along with any comments for further investigations. But these books were giving you what someone else might have done (or more likely said) hundreds or thousands of years ago. And they would take paragraphs, or pages, or sometimes even whole chapters, to say what a scientist would say in one or two sentences.

There appeared to be no rules for investigations in this area—no laws which said you had to do this or that to get results. In fact, I didn't find results from tests of any kind. No one seemed to be interested in proving or testing anything— just in endless discussions of what might have been done, or thought, or written mostly in the past. It appeared as though I was going to have to start from scratch, building for myself the tools I might need.

There were a few books by anthropologists who worked with shamans, but even they were reporting primarily what they were told, and only occasionally what they "saw." Few appeared willing to spend the many years necessary to try to become a shaman, so they could find out for themselves what might be involved here.

After more than a year of almost continuous study and meditation, initially once, and then often twice a day, I was rewarded with my first real find. The book <u>A TREATISE ON WHITE MAGIC</u> by A.A.Bailey turned out to be the guide I had been searching for. I found it in a small, local library that I suddenly just "happened" to have some time to look into. And this book also gave me the address of The Arcane School, a correspondence school teaching meditation in New York City. This school, which is based on the work of A. A. Bailey, was just what I had been searching for. At last I had someone (the school) as well as the words (the book) to help me with the beginning of my search. Now I hoped it could be conducted in a somewhat more intelligent way, rather than just thrashing about as I had been doing.

Study of many dozens of books and meditation—mostly simply sitting quietly with my eyes closed trying to "see" what would happen—continued for almost three years before I had my first mental contact with "someone." It happened as follows:

I was sitting in the garden for my usual evening meditation. I had been there for perhaps 15 to 30 minutes when suddenly there was a voice in my mind! "It" said clearly and without any introduction "Do you wish to help others or to have great wealth?" After realizing that I had just been asked a question, I mentally sent back the answer "Help others." There was no comment regarding who had asked the question or why, and there was no answer to my answer. Only afterward did I suddenly realize, with a shock, that I had received a mental communication and had automatically answered it in the same fashion, without even thinking about it! Now, more than twenty years later, I realize that if I had not answered as I had, or even taken too much time to think about which answer to give, there would have been no further communications and my long and difficult journey would have been in vain. This was just the first of many tests I was to be put to as I kept pushing on into the unknown. I didn't record the date of this transmission but it was probably late 1970, almost three YEARS after beginning my search in early 1968.

Sometime after this event (and as suggested by my correspondence school) I began keeping a journal of what I considered to be unusual thoughts or ideas that might occur during meditation. By now I was meditating at least two and often three times a day, typically 30 to 60 minutes each, every day. My meditation was no longer just sitting there, or based on someone's mantram, or using some phrase read in a book. Rather, I was guided now by what I learned in my lessons. This consisted of relaxing, mentally aligning all of my "bodies," followed by trying to quiet the mind, finally becoming "the observer," watching what the mind was doing and looking for any clues that might develop. I asked no questions since I didn't know who to address them to, or even what to ask.

Because this work was with the unknown, and since I had little idea of what might occur, all results were surprises. There were no theories to examine or to try to prove or disprove. I didn't know at the time, and still don't know today, which of the observations reported here are most important, or useful to others, and which might be worthless.

I do know that NONE of the books that I read even came close to preparing me for the startling results described later in this book.

As you read the notes of this study you will notice that there are often long gaps of many months, and sometimes even a year or more, between observations. Meditation continued during these periods. It is just that nothing that I considered interesting happened.

It wasn't until October 24, 1974, about four years after my first contact in the garden and more than six years after starting this study that I again heard a voice within. This time it was just a short statement. Another short contact happened about two weeks after that, and many more are documented later. However, it wasn't until July, 1985, 17 YEARS after I had begun my quest, that the next really startling contact occurred. That contact happened while I was in India for the second time, and will be described more fully in Chapter Four.

Deciding whether something was unusual during meditation was often difficult. By 1973 I had been meditating for about five years, and essentially nothing that I considered unusual had ever occurred other than that one contact already reported. However, from the rapidity of comments in the journal, I must have passed some kind of a milestone about that time, and now needed it to help me document what began occurring.

One of the often stated purposes of meditation is to quiet or still the mind. Unfortunately I had so far never succeeded in achieving this. My mind simply kept right on running along all through the meditation. It came up with thoughts that it wanted and ignored my desire to slow it down or stop it from generating new thoughts. I've read that this is simply a matter of will power, and that a person can stop it whenever he or she wishes. Perhaps I have an unusually active mind, or am unusually weak in attempting to stop it. But from my experience, whoever said that didn't know what they were talking about, because my mind just kept right on doing its thing no matter what I desired.

The first time that I felt that I understood this problem a little more was on May 1, 1973 when my first entry in the new journal says "Realized loose thoughts running through my mind are based on, and controlled by, the lower self." The lower self is that body that most of us consider "me," or the being that we think of as ourself. This lower self is also often called the ego. There will be more discussion of this in Chapter 9 when I describe my 45 minute contact through a channel with the Ascended Master Djwhal Khul (**DK**).

Many people are now aware that there is also a "higher self" or "Ego" that is sometimes called The Soul. This will also be discussed much more in later chapters.

The second entry occurred one day after the initial comment: "Started to reread A TREATISE ON WHITE MAGIC (for probably the second or third time) and immediately felt intense tingling throughout my skin over most of my body. This continued for some time as I read it." This tingling was to be repeated many times in the future and it seemed to be associated with something that I was supposed to do (for instance, this sometimes occurred when I was in a book store and either looking at a book, or had my hand over a book, that I should start to read). It could also indicate things I should be doing, or that some physical or spiritual change was occurring in my body. It took me years to begin to understand this effect, and I still don't fully understand what happens when it occurs.

The next entry in the journal occurred just three days later and states "Began to realize that problems I encounter are problems which I must solve and learn from." I was finding that this is a recurring theme in our existence on Earth. We are apparently on Earth to learn, and specific problems are put before us so we can learn from them. We prove by solving them that we no longer need to be exposed to that problem.

On May 8, 1973 after more than five years of work, I had a major victory! I "quieted" the brain for about 5 seconds! It IS possible. Never again did I mention this in my journal so I think this was a symbolic victory and was no longer of any importance. I could now concentrate on other things.

On May 9, 1973 I suddenly decided to begin mentally probing the interior of my body. I recorded no comments on what I saw or felt, but I apparently now felt that I had some degree of competence in controlling and directing my thoughts.

On May 11, 1973 I confirmed this by stating: "Beginning to differentiate between mental and emotional thoughts. Started to catch myself before swearing instead of afterwards."

On May 14, 1973 I started to visualize the interior of my

head by noting "Some slight pain in center of brain and tight-ness around head while visualizing head."

On May 16, 1973 I was gaining awareness of the various parts of myself when I noted "Emotional self fighting to retain freedom. Must overrule it and bring it to accept 'my' leader-ship."

An apparently important event occurred on May 18, 1973 as follows: "Just as going to sleep, a tremendous burst of light—like several flash bulbs going off in my face. This was related to a dream but I can't remember it. It did take place while in a near sleep condition, not while asleep." Several books talk about "a sudden burst of light" as starting or signify-ing some spiritual occurrence, but I was not sure exactly what happened or how it might have affected me.

On May 24, 1973 I felt that I might be able to communicate with my Soul when I "began calling on my Soul to spread light whenever undesirable thoughts crossed my mind." On June 1, 1973 I noted "this procedure is quite successful in controlling undesirable thoughts." Our lower self often generates undesir-able thoughts and it can be difficult to stop or control them. This is part of the reason why so much time was spent in attempting mind control. Asking the soul to intervene is an-other method, once some amount of mind control has been achieved.

On June 28, 1973 I had "another flash of light as I was starting to go to sleep."

By July 17, 1973 I was beginning to know the soul as I "felt the soul (?) for prolonged periods during meditation. Con-tinued on and off throughout the rest of the day."

On Dec. 12, 1973 I felt I could control the body somewhat as I was "beginning to match my body 'vibration' to the sound of AUM (or OM) when it was hummed."

By March 15, 1974 I recorded: "Seemed to have a light

above the head streaming down through much of the meditation."

This light may have had some effect, because on March 20, 1974 I was "Beginning to understand the 'oneness' of all mankind and love of all." Truly a major step forward in understanding.

On April 9, 1974 I read in one of my books that the Light comes from within and suddenly realized that I should stop trying to bring the light down from above and begin helping generate it from within. Isn't it interesting that when I apparently needed some new information, somehow I got the message of what to do? This is exactly what some of the ancient texts mean when they say: "When the pupil is ready, the master will appear." This has consistently occurred in my work although "the master" was in different forms. Sometimes it was a book, sometimes a thought or something that someone else said. It was never what I thought it would be—a robed and bearded wise person suddenly telling me what I should do.

On July 7, 1974 I recorded: "seemed to be inside the head in a great empty space looking at the inside dome of the head." Could this mean that I was empty headed, or simply that the brain isn't really the "thinker," only a mechanism?

July 16, 1974 was important because "while 3/4 asleep the Soul light (the clear light) seemed to blend with me."

On August 13, 1974 I was in New York City on business. All that evening and all night I felt intense skin vibrations. This is important because there are (at least according to some of my books) five spiritual energy input places on Earth— 1) London, England; 2) Geneva, Switzerland; 3) Darjeeling, India; 4)Tokyo, Japan; and 5) New York City. Thus, if I needed spiritual energy for some of my work, New York City would be one of the places to get it. However, I received no messages about it, just the energy.

Sept. 28, 1974 was interesting because there was no sudden insight recorded, just a feeling, with the note: "Felt at peace on waking this morning for the first time in months." It was as though I had finally accomplished something that I had been working toward for a long time. I was now beginning to wonder if we don't mentally do a lot while we are sleeping, but aren't consciously aware of it on waking up? A few of the books mention that we "are in school" during sleep, but give no specifics.

On Oct.18, 1974 a powerful insight occured. "Beginning to think of myself as pure energy." This turned out to be the beginning of a new growth stage.

Oct. 23, 1974 resulted in another powerful thought: "Realized that it is more important to spread light and love among and to others than to develop self." While this may seem basic, the concept of others being more important than self seemed to be just then developing.

On Oct. 24,1974, almost seven years after starting, I apparently did enter another phase (to which the previous ideas were just the beginning). For the first time I started waking up with very precise and clear messages in my mind. The first one said: "Let your light shine."

Apparently I tried to let my light shine with a little too much vigor, because on Nov. 5, 1974 I awoke with a second message saying: "Be more gentle in trying to become one with the light. Don't try so hard!"

The position of the "third eye," between the eyebrows, has always been an important position in the body relating to spiritual matters. It is the site of the sixth chakra. There are seven chakras in the body. A chakra is very briefly described in <u>A TREATISE ON WHITE MAGIC</u> as being "a point of latent fire." Entire books have been written on the chakras and there will be much more about them later in this book. Apparently it

CHAPTER 2

TRAVEL: TO EACH OF THE WORLD'S SPIRITUAL ENERGY INPUT LOCATIONS

My wife and I had done some travelling before my quest began to much of the Orient, East Africa, Russia, and the Scandinavian countries. These were general educational trips without a specific purpose. Now, interspersed with continued meditation and study, I began taking specific trips, alone, to many of the spiritual places on Earth. My wife was interested only in visiting "civilized" Europe and not the "wild" places I suddenly felt a need to visit.

The first of these trips, in December, 1974, was specifically designed for me to visit each of the world's spiritual energy input locations (except New York City where I had been fairly recently). This trip began in Tokyo, where, I had unexpectedly developed contacts that it would be desirable for me to meet for my consulting engineering practice. Then I was off to Calcutta, India. From there I would hop up to Nepal, and then take separate trips to Darjeeling (the second spiritual energy input location to be visited on this trip) and to Assam, before continuing to Varanasi, Lucknow, and Bombay (where I had unexpectedly also obtained consulting contacts). From Bombay I flew to Egypt, then to Greece, Switzerland (energy location no.3), and England (energy location no. 4), before returning home to California.

This was designed to be a loose trip with no hotel reservations except in Tokyo, and with flight reservations that could be easily changed. I carried only a small back pack with two additional changes of clothes. The main goal was to meditate for an hour or more, on at least one (and preferably two or three) days at each of the spiritual energy input locations. I was to be back home in about six weeks.

The stop in Tokyo proved fairly uneventful. I had been there before (17 years previously), so it wasn't the cultural shock that it can be for some. My business contacts went forward smoothly and I had about a day and a half to meditate and wander around. When I was last in New York City, as I mentioned, I had felt intense skin vibrations for more than 12 hours and I had partly expected to find the same in Tokyo. This was not the case. I felt very comfortable and relaxed, so should have been able to feel any vibrations, but there were none that I could notice.

Later in this book I will more thoroughly introduce you to my spiritual guide, with whom I am now in constant contact and who I can now ask any question I desire. I call him **DK**, and he now gives me, by direct mind to mind contact, the answer to that question. I will take advantage of this ability that I now have as I relate the notes made on this and other trips, and occasionally ask him specific questions about that trip. We will then hopefully learn together some things which I, up until this moment, have not been aware.

Question: Did I gain anything from this stop over in Tokyo?

"Yes, much more than you thought. These power input spots form a world-wide network for energy transmission to all the Earth. By stopping there you initiated a sequence of events which now allows you to direct energy to any

place on Earth as needed for the well being of Pacha Mama (DK's and The Earth's name for itself)."

Question: Did the fact that I didn't feel anything there have any significance?

"No. Your body at that time wasn't capable of detecting any of the more delicate forces that it was being subjected to, only the massive and concentrated energies of those in New York City."

Draw your own conclusions as to whether these thought transmissions are interesting and worthwhile. There will be many more of them in this book as we learn together why I did many of the things I did and giving new and fascinating bits of insight.

The trip then continued on from Tokyo to Calcutta. I actually had no interest in Calcutta. But it is the hub for air travel to almost all of north eastern India and if you are flying anywhere in this huge sector you must go through it. I was to fly into or out of Calcutta eight times on this trip.

My first destination on the second part of the journey was to be Kathmandu in Nepal. As you leave the heat, dust and humidity of the Ganges plain surrounding Calcutta, you begin to feel and see clearer air. Then, as the plane continues to climb, you are quickly over the foothills of the Himalayas. And what foothills! They are almost completely covered with terraces for growing rice. Such beauty is hard to conceive of after the shock of driving through Calcutta.

In just a few more minutes the pilot announces that you can now see Mount Everest in the distance off the right side of the airplane. The plane dipped toward the Himalayas as everyone on the left moved over to the right side to catch a glimpse of the world's highest mountain.

Before you know it you are circling to land on top of a leveled-off hill which is Kathmandu's airport. Within minutes you are thrust into the fourteenth century! It is hard to imagine a more sudden change than from a modern jet aircraft to a city that was ancient when Columbus landed in the Americas, and which has changed but little since then.

I spent three days wandering around the city and surrounding countryside. The high point of the visit was, as usual, totally unexpected. I had hiked to a large Buddhist stupa some distance from town and was wandering around the shops that surrounded it when I saw a young monk with the usual shaved head and yellow robe. For some reason I made some comment or other to him and was astounded to get an answer back in English. We immediately began talking. Imagine my surprise when I found out that this was a 23 year old American woman. She had been attending the prestigious Wellesley college in Wellesley, Massachusetts when she decided to go to Nepal and become a monk at a Tibetan Buddhist monastery that was being established on a hilltop there. We got along very well and she invited me to walk the "short" distance to her monastery.

I immediately accepted and off we went—across rice paddies, down valleys and over hills to the monastery. It was small but beautiful and was being directed by a monk who had left Tibet after the Chinese take over. The guiding force for the monastery was an American school teacher who was teaching in Kathmandu and spending all her spare time and money keeping the monastery going.

There were many occidental students there, and when the teacher found out that I was a consulting chemical engineer, I was invited by her to stay there for six months to a year. They would put me up at no cost, if I would help them solve some of their many problems. For instance their water supply was currently brought up in five gallon buckets from a nearby local stream. They also had major waste management problems, as well as problems with nearby villagers who insisted on cutting down their carefully planted trees and using them for firewood. I had to decline, but spent an absolutely delightful afternoon with them. I wrote to them for about a year afterward, giving them potential solutions to many of their problems.

From Nepal it was back to Calcutta then up to Darjeeling for the second leg of spiritual power. It is not possible to fly directly to Darjeeling. First you fly to the town of Bagdogra. Then you have the choice to either take a 12 hour cog railway ride or a six hour Jeep ride up the mountain to Darjeeling. I chose the Jeep ride because the plane's late arrival made me miss the railroad departure and I would have lost a day waiting for the next one. Darjeeling is on the very top of a mountain, with the tea estates which produce Darjeeling Tea covering much of the rest of the steep mountain side. By the time we finally arrived in Darjeeling, the mountaintop was in darkness. I asked directions to a hotel that I had read about in a guide book and fortunately it was very nearby and had a vacant room.

Early the next morning I was awakened by temple bells ringing. What a wonderful way to be awakened! I quickly dressed and followed their sound to an open area. As I slowly turned around to see where I was, there was what I think must be one of the most spectacular sights in the world! Darjeeling is right on top of a 7000 foot high mountain. What the guide books fail to mention is that from Darjeeling's mountain top you can look north to see a very deep valley—a valley that contains a good part of Bhutan. On the other side of this valley rises the third highest mountain in the world, Kantchenjunga, more than 28,000 feet in height!

As I turned around to see where I was, the sun was just rising, and my entire view was filled with this enormous mountain with its snows colored the most beautiful pink from the sunrise. Talk about a classic spiritual sight! It was breathtaking.

That view all by itself was worth the entire trip. Even today I can still feel its wonder and beauty. I must have stood there awestruck for ten minutes or more with my mouth open, I'm sure, as the sun continued to rise, producing a constant change of colors.

I finally had enough and wandered back to the hotel, which, it turned out, was really right on the top of the mountain. In fact it draped down both sides of it. I spent four glorious days there, meditating and just wandering around that mountaintop. It was cold at night (I spent New Years Day there), but the days were clear and warm and wonderful.

While this place seemed very spiritual, again I felt no particular energy inflow or presence. Just a wonderful feeling of being at peace, and enjoying the ability we now have, to travel to such spectacular places without the discomforts and time required in the past.

Riding back down the mountain, I remember most talking to my seat mate, a small, young woman from southern India who, with her husband and some friends, had come up to Darjeeling for its coolness. She had never seen snow before and I tried to describe to her what it was like to touch it—to open one's mouth when it was falling and feel its cool taste on the tongue—to be surrounded by so much of it that one could run and fall and ski in it. Until you try to describe something like that to someone who has never seen or felt it, you don't realize what a wonder many of the things on Earth really are! How privileged we should feel about being here, even for just a short stay.

Back in Calcutta I waited for my flight to Gauhati in Assam at the very northeast corner of India. Assam has been called one of the few relatively unexplored wonderlands left in the world. On arrival there (two hours late because planes don't take off in India until their landing field is clear and there was early morning fog in Gauhati), I was immediately escorted to the police station. While no specific approval is necessary to go there, I was the first westerner in years who wanted to stay in Gauhati! All others go on immediately to the nearby Kaziranga Wild Life Sanctuary.

After almost an hour's grilling by the chief of police I was introduced to the chief justice for another hour's grilling. Apparently there had been some "political activity" and officialdom wasn't taking any chances. They finally agreed to allow me to stay in Gauhati, but I was restricted to the city. My reason for going there was to visit the Hayagrib Madam Temple in Sualkuchi, 14 miles away on the other side of the huge Brahmaputra River. It is believed that Buddha attained Nirvana at this site more than two thousand years ago. I felt that such a place really wasn't outside the city, so I had my hotel clerk write down a description of where I wanted to go on a piece of paper that I could hand to the bus driver and off I went in a local bus early the next day.

In about two hours I arrived at my destination—a small village in dense jungle. After finding in which direction the temple was I finally found the hill it was on and climbed up to it. It turned out to be quite a small temple, in poor repair, with bats hanging from the ceiling in several places. I was the only visitor, but I did see a few monks around. I spent more than an hour there meditating and enjoying the peace and quiet and the lush jungle nearby.

While waiting for the bus to pick me up beside the road for my return journey, and while watching someone build themselves a new house from bamboo and palm fronds, I suddenly found myself surrounded by teenagers who, I finally figured out, wanted to know where I was from. The words "United States" meant nothing to them but they finally understood the word "America."

Finally back once again to Calcutta and then off by plane to Varanasi. What an introduction this place offers you. As you take the bus into the city, you pass more camels and elephants carrying loads of one kind or another than you do of trucks!

Varanasi, on the banks of the sacred Ganges River, is the center of the Hindu world. Just six miles away, in Sarnath, lies the center of the Buddhist world. In Sarnath, Buddha (which means "the one who is enlightened" in Sanskrit) preached his first sermon. For hundreds of years afterward there grew here a banyan tree, under which The Buddha spent "many years of meditation and purification before the final flood of light."

No one knows the age of Varanasi. It was called Kasi in the 7th century BC, but when Buddha went there in about 500 BC it was already an ancient city—perhaps older than Babylon, Nineveh, Thebes or even Jericho, which has been called "the most ancient city in the world," going back to about 8000BC.

I spent three days here just wandering around and steeping in the energies and smells and sounds of the only other city that can compare to Jerusalem as a center for more than one great religion. Strangely enough, I don't remember any particular thing that stood out, except perhaps the great numbers of people everywhere, and the brilliant colors on everything.

I took the train from Varanasi to Lucknow so I could get a better idea of this mode of travel in India. While waiting to board, an Indian trainman started talking to me and we had a wonderful half hour of conversation before the train finally pulled away. As was usual in these travels I was the only occidental in the car. The same had been true in most of the hotels I stayed in and most of the restaurants in which I ate. Quite often someone would come over, introduce themselves, and then ask if we could talk. Everywhere people wanted to know who I was, why I was there, what the rest of the world was like, and to discuss world politics. It was wonderful. What a way to discover other cultures. No set tours or conferences, just chance meetings.

In Calcutta, Varanasi, Lucknow, Deli, and Bombay I had scheduled meetings with individuals or groups to talk about a volunteer organization I often worked with in the United States. This organization, called VITA or Volunteers in Technical Assistance, was founded by several engineers at GE in the 1950's to give free technical advice and assistance abroad. As a volunteer engineer for this organization I had often provided technical information to requesters in Africa, India and elsewhere to try to help them solve problems or get new businesses started.

In Varanasi I'd had a wonderful conversation at the Gandhi Institute with an engineer. In Lucknow I was to meet with an engineer who was active in helping start up new enterprises. In Deli I had a long conversation with the Minister of Small Scale Industry. In Bombay I discussed problems with professors of mechanical engineering at the Indian Institute of Technology.

The Lucknow stopover proved interesting because not only did I meet the recently retired engineer I had expected, but also an economist from England who had recently arrived to add economics to the problem. However, what I remember most about this visit was the wonderful, very old hotel that I stayed in, the old, huge, red stone buildings and the silver foil covered cookies that I was served by the engineer's daughter while in his home.

From Lucknow I went on to Deli. I had planned to spend just two days there before going on to Kashmir. However, my travel agent had forgotten to provide me tickets for the flight to Kashmir. Also I had come down with a cold, and since the lakes in the Veil of Kashmir had just frozen over for the first time in decades, I chose not to go. This is mentioned here because one of my most profound spiritual contacts happened in Kashmir just ten years later. I now believe that it was important that I not go to Kashmir this early in my development because the energies that I would encounter at that later time would harm me if used during this early period. After looking around the area and visiting the Taj Mahal in Agra, I left for Bombay.

I had a consulting contact there, as well as the meeting at the University. After these I took a boat to the famous Elephanta caves before leaving for Cairo.

All my life I had dreamed of seeing the pyramids, the Sphinx, and the Egyptian Museum. I had even read an entire book about someone spending a night meditating in the great pyramid at Giza. The results of my visit proved less than spectacular. I felt no energies anywhere—not in the Kings chamber of the great pyramid, not standing between the paws of the Sphinx (something no longer allowed) and not in any part of the great Egyptian Museum. It was wonderful to be there, but somehow I had expected much more. I even tried to meditate in the Kings chamber because there were so few visitors there, but the young caretaker decided to spend that particular time sweeping it out. He ended up doing nothing more than raising great clouds of dust, and even worse, making continuous scratching sounds with the broom. I left Cairo two days early for Greece.

Athens was beautiful, even in the cold of January. Everywhere are spectacular monuments and pieces of ancient civilizations. Meditation was good but uneventful. I took a one day trip to the Peloponnisos peninsula and Agamemnon's grave, to try to feel the ancient flows of energy there, but felt nothing.

Geneva, Switzerland, the third of my spiritual power spots, was wonderful. Clean, cool, vibrant, and efficient (especially noticeable and appreciated after India and Egypt). I spent three delightful days there, climbing the nearby mountains, wandering the countryside, and exploring the city and lake. I was surprised not to be overwhelmed with energy there, but I felt nothing.

The flight to London was uneventful and I found a simple room in which I could meditate in peace and quiet. Again I felt no specific energy there. I left for Los Angeles a few days later.

Was this very extensive trip worth the effort? I thought it was worthwhile but was disappointed at not feeling energy anywhere. **DK** says as I write this (9/91):

"It was absolutely worthwhile and worth every minute of the time you spent both in the planning and in the doing. Because you felt nothing is unimportant. The main point of this was your commitment to try to achieve something even if you didn't know what would be the results and you felt nothing. You did something that no one had ever done before by contacting each of these points just for the specific value that might be achieved.

"We congratulate you for this very difficult and extended effort."

CHAPTER 3

MEDITATION AND TRAVEL: ENGLAND, IRELAND, SCOTLAND AND WALES, YUGOSLAVIA AND PERU

Meditation and study continued both during the spiritual power spot trip and afterwards. My lack of results that I could document from the trip did not deter me from the quest at all. If anything I felt stronger than ever about continuing. Somehow I knew that the final results—whatever they might be—would be more than worth any effort I would spend.

On May 16, 1975, three months after returning from India, I recorded a basic, but very profound, teaching: "Suddenly realized that I have two thinkers within—one, the lower self, wanting to do everything for the self. The other, the higher self, doing everything for the common good." Such a simple statement, and yet so clear and important. We each are two people, one for just ourselves, and the other thinking and working for the good of everyone, with little concern for the self. Haven't you known people who clearly show and demonstrate just one or the other? And then there are the vast majority of us who are somewhere in-between these two opposites, often sliding back and forth between them depending on the particular moment or subject, especially if we aren't directly involved?

During my July 12, 1975 meditation I followed up on this basic thought with some indication of how such vacillation or movement toward the higher self might occur: "Began to understand that the Soul or higher self overshadows the personality or ego or lower self—the personality only watching—the Soul directing. (Note: This only occurs very late in the spiritual development of the personality.)"

On driving home from work on Nov. 15, 1975 I suddenly had a very strange series of thoughts for "I suddenly felt capable of leaving Earth for good. I could now look at life 'here' with disinterest." What a strange thing to say when "here" was all I had ever known! It would be 14 more years of meditation and travel before I would learn why these thoughts happened!

On Dec. 8, 1975 I suddenly "felt light streaming out from me during meditation for the first time." What a shock that might have been, and yet, after 8 years of meditation and study there was no shock, only the careful noting that it had occurred.

The next day, on Dec. 9, 1975, I noted: "Awoke with a wonderful feeling of the presence of the illuminated mind!" Today, 16 years later, I can't remember what this felt like, but it must have been wonderful. Perhaps you, the reader, can also feel it now by sitting comfortably, relaxing in total quiet, and imagining what an illuminated mind might feel like, within your mind.

On Dec. 16, 1975, the feeling of skin vibrations over my entire body, that I had experienced only once before in New York City over a year ago, suddenly returned. How long it lasted, I didn't record, but it would probably have been during much of the meditation. The skin is the largest organ of the body and also has a huge number of nerve endings. If meditation was gradually affecting the body, perhaps this is where one would first notice that something was happening?

During January, 1976 I noted that I was fascinated by the books of Carlos Castañeda. They seemed similar to what I was attempting, except I may have had a different viewpoint and goal. Also, he had a guide and companions who were also "in training." I was trying to do it all alone, and from books (except for the comments I received monthly or quarterly through the mail from the Arcane School).

On Jan.28, 1976 I again saw bright lights within my head and noted, "Last night while going to sleep—bright lights up above as though coming through the window. Couldn't look at directly they were so bright. Saw them so clearly I touched my eyes twice to see if they were closed (they were)."

On Feb.15, 1976, I received a really startling message. "Awoke and tried to mentally align myself but suddenly received the message 'Be still and know that I am God!'."

As I write this now, **DK** is saying:

"This was your first transmission from 'The God' that we each have within us. This was a major development for you even if you didn't know it at the time."

During March 12 and again on the 14th, 1976 I noted, "Strong inflow of energy night through morning." Presumably this was the same tingling I have noted previously.

On April 2, 1976 something that I hadn't felt in a long time happened. "While meditating, my body suddenly became very still and quiet and stayed thus until meditation was complete." This is always a pleasure to have happen because the body seems to be always in such a state of agitation, even when we are sitting quietly, that one wonders if real and total quiet can ever be obtained. It can, but at least for me, not consciously or on demand.

On April 4, 1976 there was another realization. "Realized with certainty that the body is divided into three parts and the mind or higher self is totally separate and different from the lower or astral selves." Even though I realized this "with certainty," this is not quite correct. But it is close enough for someone to begin to understand that our bodies are not just one entity but a collection of energies which are guided by different intelligences with different goals and abilities. This is very difficult to define easily and we will just leave it at this for now.

On April 23, 1976 the analyst in me came out. "Suddenly realized that for many months I have been watching my thoughts carefully and examining each and trying to understand why they occur." Note no new insight, just that I caught myself doing something that I hadn't realized I was doing, and yet what I was supposed to be doing all along.

For June 2, 1976 a new mental transmission was received. "Awoke with the expression 'Breathe in energy, breathe out Love.'" This later changed to "Breathe in energy, breathe out light, and love, and power."

While driving home on June 18, 1976 I suddenly realized that "Let your light shine" means to act so it can shine. You can't force it by trying to make it shine. The word is "Let," not "Make."

On August 9, 1976 the sudden realization dawned on me that "If fear, irritation, doubt, or self-pity are bothering me then detachment is not being exercised." Detachment is one of the key things to be worked for in meditation—and in fact, during much of life. Only with detachment can one look at a problem or situation and come up with the best and most reasonable answer. Without detachment the lower self takes over and turns everything into, "what is best for me!"

Awoke on Nov. 7, 1976 with the saying, "The Lord is in his holy temple, let all the Earth be silent before Him." Some of these sayings are obviously from the Old or New Testaments and yet I hadn't been reading either of them recently. On the other hand each of them seemed to fit my current situation very well.

On November 11, 1976 while meditating and thinking, "Breathe in energy, breathe out Love," I began to actually feel

Light and Love being created within and expelled, and with each breath more and more going out. This is a wonderful feeling and again you should be able to do it by relaxing, quieting yourself and using your imagination while repeating what I was doing. Remember, this probably won't happen imediately. But with a little practice and a real desire you should be able to duplicate it and enjoy its benefits.

On November 22, 1976 I, "Awoke with the wonderful feeling of 'Oneness' With God and In Mind"

November 27, 1976 was interesting because during it I "suddenly realized that all is vibration—Love, Light, thoughts, sound, movement, energy—everything."

Dec. 15, 1976 was a continuation of this thought because during the day I, "realized that the etheric, astral, mental, solar, and monad bodies are successive, concentric shells around the physical body and they must interpenetrate and fuse over all, not at just one point or area." This may be a little difficult to picture but this thought is trying to describe our entire being, with its many levels of energy and abilities. Each shell is unique, and yet they are all part of the whole that we think of as "me." We just aren't aware of, and capable yet of utilizing, each, as we will eventually be able to do.

January 8, 1977 was a further continuation of this last thought—except that it doesn't quite agree with it. "For the entire meditation felt like I was in the Soul body and out of the physical body and able to 'look down' into the physical body (with the three sheaths)." The three sheaths is what throws me since five sheaths were just described—unless the Soul body is the fourth or solar body.

DK says: 'Yes, that is the correct interpretation."

March 25, 1977 was a big day when I had the sudden realization that, "Christ need not return as such. We are all Christ—if we wish!" This was a whole new concept for me.

We all keep wondering when The Christ, or The Lord, or Krishna, or whoever is going to return as foretold in many bibles. We also wonder where and in what form He will appear. But now I realized that The Christ is in each of us and we only need to realize this and allow this to happen. When this understanding really sinks in we can begin to teach ourselves, by whatever technique has the most meaning to us, how to allow this to happen. With me it was meditation and study.

This thought was continued three days later on March 28, 1977 when I "awoke feeling that all necessary had been done. Now I must wait with knowledge and patience."

This basic idea continued even further through most of April, 1977 when I "Had a strong input of energy each evening about 8PM or during the day when relaxing."

A new idea appeared on April 26, 1977 when I "Realized that the 'fusion force' for combining energies (contained in the many outer sheaths of the body) is through learning to properly use the vibrations contained in the sacred word 'Aum' or 'Om' or 'Amen.'"

On May 2, 1977 I began to understand how to use some of the techniques I had been learning during the last 9 years of study when, "During a bad dream, I found myself using the energies of Light and Love to counteract the effects of the bad part of the dream."

I seldom looked back in my spiritual diary to see what had been written previously. It was as though once it was written down it could then be put aside, since I had already learned it. However, on May 3, 1977, I did look back for some reason and reread "Let your light shine." "That night when reminding myself to do this, I mentally removed an encircling fence that I suddenly saw that had been preventing the Light from going forth. That fence has stayed removed so far."

Usually, when I felt an energy input, it was felt over the

entire body but most strongly in the torso. However, on May 12 and 13, 1977, I "felt the flow of energy in the palms of my hands for the first time."

On July 19, 1977 I, "Awoke feeling that I could heal." However, I didn't have any confidence in this feeling and have seldom tried to do this, not feeling that I really knew enough about it or understood it well enough to even make the attempt.

On December 19, 1977 I had an "Extraordinary awakening. A feeling of understanding of life and goals. Difficult to explain or even remember." The problem with an awakening such as this is that you end up with a wonderful feeling and knowledge of having learned or understood something profound. But as you try to relive it, to more fully grasp it and put it to use, you can't remember it well enough to make it useful. Furthermore, within minutes of writing down what you do remember, even that little bit starts to disappear. This has happened so many times that I have begun to believe very strongly that when we are sleeping we really are in a class somewhere, trying to grasp the lessons that we exist for.

On February 9, 1978, about ten years after beginning this study, I "Realized that the Light within can be used as a shield to help block out unwanted thoughts." Unwanted thoughts have always been a problem, and much of my initial meditation was spent in trying to block them out or better yet, prevent them from forming in the first place. But I now see that this is a brute force approach. A much more refined and delicate approach is to use Light with your mind to block them out.

Another step forward occurred during April, 1978 when I "Began visualizing instead of enunciating thoughts and ideas during meditation." It was now obvious to me that thinking in words is not nearly as effective or complete or descriptive as visualizing thoughts. Words are too restrictive and limiting since they demand a well understood vocabulary and are based on a local culture. Visualizing thoughts surmounts these restrictions and adds a whole new dimension and beauty to communication. The only problem is that one must be in mind contact with another for this to occur.

This is possible!

In fact, we sometimes do it without realizing it when we suddenly feel intense emotions such as love or hate. Unfortunately, when we allow the emotional body to take over, we initiate other problems and lose the control that is so necessary for mind contact to be really useful and meaningful. The comments that I have mentioned from **DK** so far have come through direct mind contact. More on this later.

On April 1, 1979, after an entire year without any further input, I suddenly "Awoke with the strong feeling that I was to be a transmitter of Power, Light, and Love for the Spiritual Hierarchy."

As I write these words, **DK** (a member of this organization) is giving me a description of this group.

"The Spiritual Hierarchy, sometimes called The Brotherhood, is a spiritual organization which interacts with God to carry out plans for the growth of mankind as laid down at the formation of the Earth. Members are typically not physically present on Earth, although they may occasionally take a physical form by incarnating on Earth for a particular life time and time period. As explained later in this book they typically work through individuals on Earth by placing situations or ideas before carefully selected individuals and then step back to see what happens. In this manner they attempt to guide the growth of mankind and help it to—when ready—progress up the ladder of spiritual development. But this is always done without taking away any of mankind's inalienable right of self-determination."

After this last input, for some reason I stopped writing in the journal until June 1988, almost ten years later and twenty years after I began the quest. Study and meditation continued but, apparently, nothing happened to make me want to dig out the journal to add to it. During this time I moved from California to New Hampshire, began a new job, and designed and built a new and strange house. It was a square, underground house with a pyramid roof instead of covering it with earth. The two floors in the above ground pyramid were designed as a separate and complete house as was the underground portion. We planned to live above ground in the beautiful Spring and Fall, and underground in the cold Winter and hot Summer. Unfortunately, it didn't work out quite that way because my wife didn't care to live underground, though I felt very comfortable there. Accordingly we each lived in our prefered section of the house, meeting for meals and evenings. I also took additional trips to many spiritual places around the world during this time. Apparently I had begun a totally new phase of work which was more concerned with physical movement and action than the mental development which had been going on for the previous ten years. Discussions of some of these new happenings follow.

June, 1982: Traveled to Ireland, England, Scotland and Wales. This trip was not to try to find or feel anything, or to go any place in particular. Rather it was to continue the learning process already begun about the many peoples and places on the Earth—to try to develop a more global understanding.

This was a very low-key, low-cost, trip with a large group of teachers. We were taken to major population centers and then left on our own, to go where we wanted. Ireland was much more beautiful and lush and green than I expected, Wales more stark, but beautiful in its own way, and Scotland very special, with its wonderful museums and antiquities. I would later make a whole trip just to Scotland to add to this experience. Stonehenge was as spectacular as I hoped but there was no feeling of energy near it. I had been to the British Museum before but a another visit is always a special occasion. All in all, a great trip but with nothing that really stands out as unique or important.

In October, 1983, I went to Yugoslavia to take care of some family business. I was trying to find the wonderful person who had loaned my wife enough money so she could return to the United States after being trapped there throughout World War II. I found him on my last day there and the money—now a very considerable sum because of its growth in a bank over a 30 year time period—allowed him and his wife to "live like royalty" in his retirement. The trip turned out to be a great success, not only because I was able to find the person involved, but because it allowed me to become familiar with such a different part of Europe with its very special and difficult ethnic problems. It has so many different cultures, languages, alphabets, hates and religions all jammed together in such a small area—a true microcosm of the Earth within a few thousand square miles.

February, 1984: This time to Peru. It was another low cost, easy trip. We were taken to a population center (Lima in this case) and left on our own. I traveled to Cuzco, Ollantaytambo, and Pisac in the Andes, and Iquitos on the Amazon. I had a great time, and enjoyed the trip thoroughly, but this was my exploratory trip here and there were no feelings of having been here before or of unusual power happenings. I would go here again several years later with a Peruvian shaman. Peru would then truly become a wonderland of energy, insight and development. Many pages in this book will be devoted to this later, very powerful trip.

It will be noted that several of the trips described here and later did not provide any sudden insight or feeling of spiritual growth. Rather they resulted more in a gradual growth in understanding of the Earth, its peoples and its cultures, so that in the future I could react more knowingly in attempting to solve problems that I might be involved in. The greatest part of my spiritual insight and wisdom was received after this second ten year period of study, travel, and meditation and after I had largely stopped traveling.

CHAPTER 4

TRAVEL: BALI & SRI LANKA,
THE HIMALAYAS & LADAKH,
& SCOTLAND

In September, 1984 I left for the islands of Bali and Sri Lanka with a stop in Korea and Singapore both ways. The purpose of this trip was to compare the cultural effects of the almost pure Buddhist religion of Sri Lanka, with the strange and wonderful religion of Animism (or nature worship) combined with Hinduism, unique to Bali. Since these are two of the oldest religions on Earth, I was curious to see what effects they might have on the way the cultures had developed and on the happiness of the people.

While I obviously couldn't do an in depth study in just the two weeks I was there, I had studied each of the religions over a period of years and was really looking more for general impressions rather than for a precise comparison.

These islands are among the most beautiful on Earth. Each has wonderful coast lines, jungles, mountains and wildlife. The people of both are friendly and appear to be largely content with their way of life. In general, the population of Bali seemed to be more at ease with nature and their Gods than in Sri Lanka.

There appeared to be no major difference in general attitude or success (however you might wish to define it), especially when considering that each had followed only one religion for well over a thousand years. Perhaps religion doesn't affect cultures as much as one would like to think. Perhaps, instead, attitudes toward each other and toward the Earth permit acceptance of religion. This religion is then modified to become acceptable to a general population—rather than vice versa?

Everywhere I have been, it seems that the environment itself—desert or jungle, cold or hot, much or little food— appears to have had much more effect on the people than any particular religion. And further, religions that have been generally accepted, or developed locally, seem to permit the population to fit into its environment with relative ease rather than attempting to overcome or alter it. Perhaps we need religions only to give us a way to deal with questions about God and death, and to suggest how to get along with each other?

Even with so much beauty around me, I felt no particular energy or spiritual thoughts on either island. I left, happy to have seen such beautiful places, but without feeling any noticeable inspiration or spiritual growth.

I had loved the Himalayas while I was in Nepal and India, and had been a student of the Tibetan form of Buddhism for many years. When I "happened" to pick up a book in a local book store on speculation of where Christ might have spent the years between the ages of about twelve and about thirty, I was fascinated to find that there was some indication that HE might have spent at least some of those years in northern India, Ladakh, and Tibet. One of the particular locations mentioned was the Himis (or Hemis) Monastery near Leh, Ladakh. I therefore decided to explore the possibilities of going there to see what might occur. I had originally planned to go to Tibet, but entry had to be from China in 1984-85. No one was allowed across the Nepalese border into Tibet then, and for some reason I didn't wish to go in through China. Eventually I found that one of the trekking groups from Boston was planning a trek across part of the Himalayas and into Ladakh. In July, 1985, six of us left the U.S. to make this journey.

This was planned to be a very spiritual journey for me. (For the others it was apparently a purely physical experience.) It turned out to be much more than I expected. We left Boston on July 16 and arrived in Srinigar, Kashmir, India during the afternoon of July 18, after an exhausting flight, with two plane changes and several hour layovers in London and Delhi. We were to spend about two days in Srinigar (at about 5000 feet elevation) so we would become more acclimatized to the altitude, since we would be trekking at elevations in the 10,000 to 16,000 foot range.

About 2AM in the morning of the 19th I suddenly awoke starved for food. I couldn't understand this because we had been very well fed on the airplane and in Delhi and Srinigar. Fortunately, one of the women I worked with in the US had given me about a pound of cookies she'd made for me. I got up and ate one, then another and another until they were all gone—something unheard of for me since I seldom ate more than two or three cookies at a time.

I mention this here because something had made me extremely hungry, even though I shouldn't have been, and this hunger woke me, kept me awake and proved to me that I was awake (because all the cookies were gone in the morning). Immediately after eating all those cookies and going back to bed I suddenly began to shiver, even though it was a warm and comfortable night. I shivered violently for perhaps five minutes, then tears began to flow—in great quantities—and continued for many more minutes. Then, all of a sudden, there were words forming in my mind! These words felt quite different from any that I had heard before. These words were not heard. They were not seen. They were just there! And they were words, not pictures. The words were as follows:

"You were one with another many centuries ago.

"Contact was lost.

"We are one again.

"Contact will not be lost again."

What did it mean? I had no idea. I did write it down immediately after it stopped, however, so it wouldn't be forgotten. Twenty four hours later the same thing happened again, except that this time I was just awakened, there was no hunger (a good thing too, because I didn't have any more cookies to eat!) Again I spent perhaps five minutes shivering and again the tears flowed copiously. Then again the words were there. This time they said simply:

"The reason for this incarnation is completed."

No more. No hints as to what it might mean or what I was to do about it. As I thought about it over the weeks, months and years that followed I finally reached the following conclusions:

1) This was probably my Soul which contacted me and was definitely not the entity or entities that had contacted me before. It felt totally different.

2) If the Soul wished to contact the conscious body it would be done in such a way that a) you would know that it wasn't a dream, b) it was to be remembered and therefore should be written down exactly as transmitted immediately after the transmission stopped, c) it would utilize involuntary bodily functions such as hunger, shivering, and tears that typically are not controlled by the conscious person so that the person knows something very special is happening.

3) Words are transmitted directly to the brain without the use of either sight or sound, unlike the way information is usually transmitted to the conscious individual.

4) The contact is to achieve some very specific purpose which probably will not have any direct meaning to the individual or require any conscious action—other than a great deal of thinking and wonder.

Why am I now sure that this "contact" was the Soul? Because I asked **DK** while I was writing this book (9/91) to confirm these previous conclusions. His answer was as follows:

"Because the feeling that you have about this occurrence is one of beauty and pleasure as well as curiosity. There is no fear or concern involved. And because there is nothing required of you to do. This is very important. The Soul will NEVER tell you to do something or carry out some service. This contact will usually indicate that at some later date you can be of some use to the Spiritual Hierarchy if you wish, but it will be entirely up to you and the opportunity to serve may be many years away."

The two days spent in the Veil of Kashmir in and around Srinigar were wonderful. It truly is one of the most beautiful places on Earth, with huge lakes and a fertile valley surrounded by very high and picturesque mountains as well as an ancient race of people.

During my first trip to India I developed a quick method of determining if there was what we think of as poverty in a particular location. This consisted of asking myself three simple questions. First, did the children seem to be full of energy and were they happy and laughing (indicating an adequate diet and home life)? Second, were there pets around (indicating excess food)? Third, were there sellers of candy and cookies on many of the streets (indicating excess money)? If these three criteria were met, I felt this particular culture was doing OK. I have never been anywhere where these three criteria were not met (except in rural parts of countries where there are seldom sweets vendors).

After this wonderful start to the trip, the rest of it was really an anticlimax. However, the days spent trekking were wonderful and very spiritual in their own way. The mountains, glaciers and valleys covered with wildflowers were beautiful. One thinks of these mountains as being stark and totally covered with snow. Rather they were lush with grasses, trees, bushes, and wildflowers everywhere. Many places we walked through were well above the tree line but even here there were beautiful flowers and streams among the rocks. And there were many more local people in the valleys and on steep hillsides than I expected—whole families sometimes, and other times shepards who were tending their flocks of sheep.

After six days of hiking and camping between mountains and next to icy glacier streams, at elevations in the 11000 to 14000 foot range, we descended to a small village where cars were waiting to complete the journey into Ladakh. Since there is only a very narrow, one way road to Ladakh, and the military use it all day long to bring supplies that must last throughout the winter, to the towns, it is necessary to wait until dark for them to finish before you can proceed.

Unfortunately there were many landslides covering parts of the road this year so the military was using it during the night time as well as during the day. We ended up waiting 30 hours at the road's beginning before we could proceed. The first leg of the drive—when we finally did get going—was finished in total darkness and completed the crossing of the Himalayas. We stopped at the village of Kargil early the next morning to give the drivers some sleep. Fortunately we could now drive in daylight, since the road widened a little, but there were still mud slides everywhere. We often found ourselves inching over mud or taking off into the fields to get around a larger slide which totally closed the road.

Ladakh is a totally different world from Kashmir. This is very high desert, varying in altitude from about 10,000 feet to well over 20,000 feet, with one of its PASSES at 17,800 feet. Unless you are at the bottom of a river valley, with its lower elevation and water, there is no plant life visible.

Ladakh has been called by some "mysterious and archaic," by others "little Tibet" and by still others "the moon land" or "the last Shangri La." It is the most remote region of India (more so even than Assam) and is an essentially barren, rainless area north of the Himalayas. It is included in that area known as the Tibetan Plateau. Access is limited to just two or three months of the year since it is usually about July before the snow melts sufficiently to allow ground transport. An airline flies in when not restricted by weather—which is much of the time. Whatever you call it, it is totally different from any other place on Earth.

Our first stop on the way to Leh, the capital city, from Kargil was Mulbekh monastery (or Gompa) with its nearby, 20-30 foot tall figure of the Matriya (future Buddha) cut into the rock. This figure is believed to date from around the time of the birth of Christ—a great symbol to start a new adventure.

After going over one pass (Lamika La) at 12,080 feet, and a second (Fatu La) at 13,300 feet we descended slightly to Lamayuru Gompa. Talk about Shangri La personified! Here was a large monastery perched right on top of a mountain peak. In the valley below it were green fields and tall trees along with a beautiful river. This Gompa was built around the 10th century.

There weren't many monks around during our stop but I had a feeling of energy here.

It was late in the afternoon when we finally drove into Leh to find our hotel rooms. The next day we took jeeps and went Gompa hopping. First to Shey Gompa, then to Hemis Gompa that I had come so far to see. Hemis Gompa itself could never have been visited by Christ since it wasn't built until the 17th century. However, such structures are often built over, or next to, previous holy structures. Further, a book in its library is thought to be a copy of the original (in a monastery at Marbour near Lhasa) which is reported to discuss both Moses (Mossa) and a Saint Issa which may be the local name given to Christ.

While such reports are interesting, I had no way of translating such texts, even assuming that I could gain access to them. Therefore I had decided to go there to try to sense and become one with any energies that might have developed over hundreds or thousands of years of prayer by Buddhists, Hindus, Christians, or those of the earliest religion of Bon (nature worship). Hemis was essentially deserted on the day we were there, most of the monks being away on a trip, but we were allowed to wander fairly freely through the buildings and their main prayer room. This room was wonderful. Dark, low ceilinged, with pillows to sit on—it was full of energy. Even I, with my limited development and abilities, could feel it there. I would have loved to have spent a year there, or at least taken part in a few prayer ceremonies. Such was not to be, however, and I accepted this with ease. I had long ago learned that everything happens for the best and to stop fretting when things don't go as you think they should.

We spent about two hours there. On the way back to Leh we stopped at Tiksa Gompa, but I was by now too emotionally stimulated and physically tired (Leh is at an altitude of about 11,500 feet, everywhere else typically somewhat higher) to hike up to its hilltop buildings. Instead I spent some time with a four year old monk with his rubber boots, shaved head and red robe. We communicated by just sitting together and sometimes moving our arms or hands for emphasis.

The next day the other five went on another three day trek

while I stayed behind to enjoy this unreal place. I'd had some difficulties hiking (either from not drinking enough water while hiking or from lack of oxygen) while we were waiting to drive up to Leh and I wasn't interested in going much higher. Further, I really didn't want to leave Leh. There was just too much to see and feel and do here. These wanderings and meditations went by all too fast, and before I knew it it was time to fly back to Srinigar. This was, however, not as simple as it seemed. The single daily flight had not been able to fly into Leh for two days previously because of bad weather over the Himalayas and all the passengers from those canceled flights wanted to leave on our plane. The rules are very strict on this here. Those booked on the current flight get their seats. All others must wait to see if any more are available. Incidentally the cars we had come up on were standing by for us in case our plane was also cancelled. There were lots of shouts about "Do you know who I am," etc. but we got our seats!

The flight back was absolutely spectacular. Almost the entire flight time was spent over the Himalayas—one huge mountain after another until you lost all track of their number. There were two more days (held in reserve in case we had to drive back) in Srinigar and then home. This was the most powerful trip I had been on by far. Truly remarkable!

In August, 1986 I left for Scotland to spend an entire week just driving around this ancient land. I had decided to go after I saw a picture of The Standing Stones of Callanish on the Isle of Harris and Lewis in the Outer Hebrides. This ancient stone structure is one of the largest and best preserved in the United Kingdom, after Stonehenge. It looked to me far older than Stonehenge because its stones are so much cruder and smaller—as though technology hadn't yet made a Stonehenge possible.

Landing in Scotland was no problem but getting my rental car to go was. The car was a manual shift model with four forward gears. It had been many years since I had driven a manual shift car and I couldn't get it into reverse to even get out of the parking lot. Not an auspicious beginning, I must say. After fully fifteen minutes of trying every trick I knew, and working up a sweat over it, I finally, vaguely remembered reading somewhere that you had to push down on the shifter before it would go into reverse! Sure enough, it worked and I was off. The next challenge was driving on the left side of the road. This appeared to be no problem because I had mentally prepared myself for it. Unfortunately I hadn't prepared myself to make a right or left turn into traffic. I had some close ones and could see the approaching drivers swearing at me as I switched from one lane to another trying to see which side someone going my way was driving on. To this day, I still break out into a sweat just trying to figure out where I ought to be in a left or right turn.

Following this very shaky start I spent the rest of the day driving to the mystical Isle of Skye from the airport at Prestwick. Day two was spent driving around the Isle of Skye as I waited for the ferry for the four hour ride to the Isle of Harris and Lewis. Once there I drove from the ferry port of Tarbert to the Isle of Lewis (it is one island, the south part is Harris, the north part is the Isle of Lewis) and its seaport, and only major town, Stornoway.

I spent the third day just wandering among the many ancient stone monuments on the Isle of Lewis. There are many of them and they are still finding more! But the Standing Stones at Callanish are very special. For one thing, they are not in the form of a circle as is Stonehenge or in radiating lines as are the Carnac stones of Brittany and Hill O'Many Stones in Scotland (which I also visited—in a driving rain). These stones at

Callanish are in the form of a cruciform or cross—radiating out to the North, East, South, and West.

I tried, without success, to feel any energies or get any guidance here, though I touched most of the stones and walked along their radiating arms. But, while this would have been nice, it wasn't necessary. Just being there and seeing this visually powerful work of art and religion was enough.

Actually, as so often happens on these trips, the thing I remember with the greatest pleasure was not these stones but a special two hour service of the Free Church of Scotland, in Stornoway, on a Friday evening, into which I just happened to wander. The service was all in Gaelic so I didn't understand a word, but the music, sung by the congregation, was heavenly. I think that this is the most beautiful church music I have ever heard. They only sang three times but that was enough. Tears rolled down my cheeks as they sang, it was so hauntingly beautiful.

On returning to the mainland I continued my trip around the northern and eastern periphery of Scotland, stopping at many ancient sites and cairns along the way. I had hoped to be able to catch the ferry at Scrabster, to go further north to see the ancient sites on the Orkney Islands, but missed the ferry by two hours and couldn't wait a day to catch another.

After reaching Inverness I continued east to the spiritual retreat at Findhorn. Unfortunately, the person in the office there was very unhelpful, offering no suggestions, either for finding a place to stay for the night, or about the activities there. I spent just a short time looking around and then drove back toward Inverness to find lodging, before continuing around Scotland's periphery.

It was a fairly fast trip, driving 1350 miles in 7 days, plus travel on three ferries, but there were many stops along the way that I haven't mentioned. Scotland is a beautiful and mystical place. I felt most at home there, and very much enjoyed the monuments and the people. I believe that I gained something ethereal from the visit, but I can't describe it more exactly than that.

CHAPTER 5

TRAVEL: THE YUCATAN AND COSTA RICA

In October, 1986, I flew to the Yucatan Peninsula of Mexico to explore some of the many Mayan temples there. Within minutes after landing at Cancun I was driving through dense jungle on my way to the ruins of Chichen Itza.

I had seen my first ancient ruins in 1948 when two friends and I drove to Mexico City (from Colorado) during the Christmas break of our last year in college. I can still remember how impressed I was with Teotihuacan, just outside Mexico City. Very little restoration work had been done at that time—it seemed almost more a pile of rocks than anything else—but it was so large and the ruins so high! Actually this is one of the most impressive complexes of ruins in the world. Its name, incidentally has been translated as "Place where man becomes a god" or "Place where the Gods touch the Earth." (Aren't these translations wonderful and descriptive? However, they state quite different ideas. Which is right? **DK** says the latter is more nearly correct, but even it isn't exact!) This site covers about 9 square miles! In any case, even with that beginning, I wasn't prepared for Chichen Itza, at least part of which has been largely restored.

Chichen Itza (meaning "near the fountain of the Itza people") is one of the largest and best restored of the many archeological sites in Mexico. You have a feeling of great awe and wonder when you first walk into this or one of the many other sites—even more so than I felt in Egypt, walking up to the pyramids and the Sphinx, or in India where the large, ancient buildings are fewer and more widely spread out. Here the pyramids and buildings are huge, and there are so many of them. This particular site covers about 3 square miles, and, as on almost all pre-Columbian sites, it has been only partly excavated.

This site was founded about 450 AD and was abandoned about 1200AD. Chichen Itza was a sacred site and was built with strict astronomical and astrological considerations. For instance, the tallest building, El Castillo, is a pyramid over 80 feet tall (taller than an 8 story building). It has nine terraces and four staircases believed to symbolize the nine heavens and the four points of the compass. Each staircase has 91 steps making a total of 364. If you then include the final summit platform as one step you have 365, the number of days in the year.

This pyramid rises at an angle of about 45 degrees and while it is somewhat difficult to climb up because of the steepness, it's really frightening to have to climb down. All you see is space out in front of you and it feels like it is going almost straight down. Most adults, including myself, tend to back down it, at least the first time.

What a wonderful place to explore, though! On every turn there is something new to discover and investigate. Once you complete the restored section, there is the partly restored section, with its "observatory" among many other buildings, to wander around and wonder at. And if you are still curious you can hire a guide, as I did, and go out into the jungles for much, much more to see, including some of the native wildlife. At one building the guide would only take me within a few hundred yards of it. He said the last time he was there, several weeks before, there was a very large rattlesnake in its courtyard and he really wasn't interested in encountering it in the high brush we would have to walk through to get closer! Further, as I walked back along a narrow jungle trail, following him by a distance of about five feet, I suddenly saw a large snake hurry across the trail between us. When I yelled a warning to him, his reply was "what color?" I said "a beautiful brown with black stripes." He turned white and replied "Oh! Very poisonous!."

There is so much in just this one site that you can hardly grasp it all. For instance, in one of the outlying buildings called the "Church," among much ornamentation, and between Chac masks, are carved a prawn, an armadillo, a snail and a turtle. These are the four lifeforms which support the sky in Mayan mythology—certainly an interesting combination of animals.

I loved Chichen Itza and felt very much at home there. I spent my first day and a half there, and then returned for another day, later in the week, just to sit and meditate. There were no specific feelings of energy there, just a wonderful sense of well being.

From Chichen Itza I drove to the nearby sacred cave of Balankache. It's entrance is quite deep, narrow and warm. Furthermore there is a very limited supply of air in the cave because it has only the one opening into it. You're sure that you are using all the air as you struggle up and down the path inside the cave. In fact, about every hundred yards or so I had to stop for almost five minutes to fully catch my breath. It was worth it to get into the final chamber of worship, but I wouldn't recommend it to anyone out of shape, afraid of close spaces or with a limited breathing capacity!

While driving to the next site of Dzibichaltun I noticed an arrow pointing to another archeological site and drove the fifteen miles of bad roads to it. It was fascinating. This site hadn't even been given a name that I could discover, I guess because there were so many other, larger sites nearby. Yet anywhere else on Earth these ruins would have been world class. On top of a hill was a very large structure perhaps a hundred or more yards long and thirty or forty feet wide with more than twenty carved columns still remaining. As I was walking back I came across a troupe of girl scouts walking to the area, so it wasn't being entirely ignored.

The trip to Dzibichaltun (translated "where the flat stones bear writing") then continued. These ruins aren't nearly as easy to find, as spectacular, or as well rebuilt as Chichen Itza, but they certainly are large. It would have been easy to get lost in them. There are TWENTY SQUARE MILES of ruins in this complex. This is the largest known Mayan site, with more than 8000 buildings, and was obviously an important ceremonial center. This site had the usual cenote or sacred well. However, out of this one alone 30,000 archeological items have been recovered! I was caught in a sudden, powerful rainstorm here and spent a half hour standing inside an ancient carved gate to keep dry. What symbolism, waiting in a gate—to where?—complete with rain to wash away past transgressions!

From this site I drove on to the town of Merida to stay overnight. I left early the next morning for Uxmal (pronounced Ushmal and meaning "the thrice built.") This site is one of the finest and most complete complexes of pre-Columbian architecture in all of Mexico, begun in about the 6th century.

The first thing you see on entering this site is a strange and very large pyramid about 125 feet high. This pyramid is not only very tall, but is very steep, with sides sloping at about 60 degrees. It is so steep, in fact, that after I climbed the first few steps I stopped, looked around, and then immediately crawled backwards back down. It would really have been frightening to try to come down from any greater height!. This is the only pyramid I have ever seen, anywhere, that has ROUNDED corners! It is really quite startling to see for the first time. It even carries this rounding effect to its base which is oval instead of square.

It's interesting that as advanced as the Mayans were, in their calendar and their highly decorated buildings, they never developed the curved arch which is so basic to most western architecture. Instead they used corballing, or overlapped stones, with each succeeding layer being placed a little closer to the center. This method of construction is sometimes also called a false arch. This meant that wide rooms were difficult to construct or required a very high ceiling. In fact, the first thing you note on entering the buildings—in addition to the bats that are everywhere—is the narrowness of the rooms and entryways because of this design.

There is another very interesting building here called the Great Pyramid. This is the only pyramid I have ever seen built into a natural hill. There is stone structure on only one side of the hill, with the other three sides being natural hill. It is a beautiful blending of nature and the works of man. I enjoyed this site, but didn't feel the warmth here that I enjoyed so much at Chichen Itza.

It was only 12 miles or so to my next stop at Kabah. Imagine one complex after another, few of them more than twenty or thirty miles apart. What a civilization this must have been a thousand to fifteen hundred years ago! And to think that it just disappeared about 1200 AD! No one knows for sure why. Most probably from a great drought.

As I write this **DK** is saying:

"It was from a combination of many factors. Their religion was failing, there were too many people and too many wars, the weather was changing so they were having crop failures and many other smaller problems, all conspiring to create difficulties that their leaders or 'control

centers' couldn't handle or resolve. The people just stopped coming to these spectacular religious centers. Some drifted away to where they could find an authoritarian leader, others just stayed in their homes until things got somewhat better. By that time there was no more 'civilization' left that needed these structures."

(Doesn't **DK** provide a knowledge and insight totally unobtainable from anywhere else?)

Kabah was interesting but had no special features that intrigued me so I drove on to Edzna (meaning "house of grimaces") which covers about 2 1/2 square miles. There was little here that interested me, except for a pyramid called "The Five Story Building" which had rooms in the first four stories—something I had never seen before. It also had what was to become familiar in buildings at many sites—a "roof-comb" 20 feet high. No one seems to know what this strange structure is for. It would be perhaps ten or fifteen feet long, three to five feet wide, and fifteen to twenty-five feet high, and be essentially a series of close together, square or rectangular pillars, connected together at their base, reaching up to the sky. There would be no roof on these columns. The total height of this pyramid including the comb is about 100 feet.

(**DK** is saying:

"These structures were designed to represent mankind's hand or hands reaching toward God in the sky and asking for help and love and protection!")

From Edzna I drove to the town of Campeche on the Gulf of Mexico to spend the night. My first stop the next day was to be Sayil which means "place of the ants." Sayil had only one really interesting building for me, a Palace with three floors, each one set back from the others so there was a garden or terrace around each. Sounds like some of our modern buildings, doesn't it? From Sayil I drove on to Xlapak then on to

Labna (meaning "broken houses" in Mayan).

The most interesting structure in Labna was a superb structure called the Arch of Labna, a structure faintly resembling the Arch de Triomphe in Paris. Then I visited Chunyaxche, a site still pretty much buried in the jungle. I finally gave up for the day at the town of Akumal on the Caribbean Sea having completely crossed the Yucatan Peninsula this day.

The first stop the next day was Tulum, the only known Maya fortified town located on the coast. The name of Tulum is appropriate because it means "fortress" in Mayan. I found it interesting primarily because of its beautiful location rather than any structures there. From Tulum I went on to Coba which means "Wind ruffled water" probably because it is between two large lakes, something very unusual in the Yucatan. Coba is the oldest known ceremonial center in the Yucatan and, probably because of its abundance of water, was occupied from about 300 AD to about the 15th century, longer than any other site in this region. It is also one of the largest Mayan sites, covering about 18 square miles. So far about fifty roads and more than 6000 buildings have been discovered here. Some of these roads are more than 30 feet wide and are surfaced with a limestone that is almost like concrete. One is almost 65 miles long! It must have been a magnificent city. Unfortunately few buildings have been reconstructed so far.

The most interesting structure at Coba is the pyramid called El Castillo, 138 feet (fourteen stories) high, and the highest accessible ancient structure in the Yucatan. There are also several stelae (or carved stones) here—something that is not often seen at these sites any more since they are small enough to be easily removed to local museums.

From the top of El Castillo you not only have a magnificent view of the surrounding jungles, but you also can see many other pyramid tops poking up through the jungle canopy. A few have been partially cleaned off, most are still totally covered with vegetation.

Finally I returned to Chichen Itza for another visit before returning to Cancun for the flight home.

Four months later I was again flying south, this time to Costa Rica. This trip was not so much to see man made wonders as to feel Earth energies in the jungles, rain forests, and active volcanoes.

Costa Rica proved to be an even more beautiful country than I expected—quiet, peaceful and concerned about its citizens—where you are first surrounded by, and then engulfed in, nature.

The first side trip was north to the active volcano of Poas. The trip proved to be as interesting as the volcano itself. Coffee plantations are everywhere (between 3000 and 7000 foot altitudes), along with sugar cane fields, wild bamboo, strawberry fields, cut flower fields and bromiliads growing wild in the trees. The volcano itself was most interesting with its recently scarred slopes, and with smoke and steam rising from the current vent.

Next was a wonderful guided car trip down the mountain, from the capitol of San Jose to the Pacific Ocean, to visit a "dry" jungle at the Carara Biological Reserve. This is a fascinating place—a true jungle with little rain, right along the Pacific Ocean. Costa Rica has about 20% of its land in National Forests and Reserves vs about 2% in the U.S. Still there is pressure to put even more in such reserves.

At one place during our walking tour, we stopped to look at a snake that had frozen in position on a bush at the edge of the trail. Then another, different species of snake, started coming toward us on the ground. Since I was closest to it , the guide said "don't move!" This snake proceeded to move over my shoe, then finally away as he continued on his way. He seemed totally oblivious to my being there. Afterwards, the guide noted that he was a relatively harmless type!

The next day I was on another tour going south to the active volcano of Irazu—with quite different landscapes this time but just as interesting. The fourth trip was to Lankestar Gardens, a few miles from San Jose. This garden specializes in orchids, both native and imported, which they grow totally outdoors over acres of ground. It's a wondrous place if you're interested in these spectacular plants.

The next day I was up early to catch the train to Puntarenes, a port city on the Pacific Ocean. I had seen this area before on the ride down to the dry jungle, but I wanted to go by train this time, to meet more people. I also wanted to stay overnight just a few feet from the Pacific Ocean.

This trip was interesting if uneventful, and I arrived back in San Jose, again by train, the next day without incident. The following morning I was up early again to catch another train, this time to Port Limon on the Caribbean. This trip, was totally different because it was almost entirely through thick jungle, while the previous trip was mostly over grasslands. Furthermore, while the first trip had only a few stops, this one stopped about 50 times! There were many banana plantations to see but the most interesting thing there was the clean up squad I met early the next morning on the city streets—huge vultures. They were everywhere, picking up scraps left over from the previous night.

I returned to San Jose by bus stopping along the way— often near fruit stands with their five or six varieties of mangos, fresh pineapples, bananas and citrus fruit of all kinds.

DK says, as I write this:

"The active volcanoes bring the energy of the inner Earth to the surface, and near them their 'unusual' kind of energy can be tapped into—something that is desirable for

someone who is striving to control energy."

DK's comments as I write this book are fascinating to me because I often had little or no idea exactly WHY I was taking these trips. Usually I just suddenly developed a curiosity about a particular place.

CHAPTER 6

TRAVEL: EGYPT AND THE HOLY LAND

When I was first in Egypt, in 1975, I only spent three days there and wasn't too impressed with what I saw. There were too many people pushing you for "baksheesh" and Cairo's crowds were everywhere. Also on that trip, I still had several other destinations yet to go, so Cairo became more of a stop-over than an objective, although the pyramids, Sphinx and Egyptian Museum were wonderful to explore.

For this second visit I was traveling with a small group so I wouldn't have to be concerned about anything but learning from the trip. I had selected the particular trip with care so it would take me almost everywhere I wanted to go without further work on my part. And there were others along to inter-act with—something that I thought might be interesting after my last few solo trips.

This trip started in April, 1987, beginning in Egypt, and was completed during May with travels in the Holy Land. This time, for some reason, Cairo appeared much more friendly. It was even more crowded, but somehow no one seemed to be pushing as hard as last time. Perhaps I was more prepared for it, or just wasn't concerned about anything but learning and growing from what I saw and felt.

The trip began with a short ride to the ancient city of

Memphis, 14 miles south of Cairo. For a city that was the glory of Egypt since the beginning of its recorded history, very little remains. Memphis was on the border between the two ancient kingdoms of Upper and Lower Egypt and was where most of the early pharaohs lived. It held an important place in Egypt throughout much of its early history, flourishing during the Old Kingdom and continuing in importance during the Middle and New Kingdoms. Today there is essentially nothing there. A single modern building to house a statue of Ramesses II with a large alabaster sphinx sitting outside, is about all.

From Memphis we traveled to the Step Pyramid at Saqqara. This was the cemetery for ancient Memphis (the cemeteries in ancient Egypt were mostly on the west or setting-sun side of the Nile) and it is generally believed that this pyramid of Zoser or Djoser (from the 3rd Dynasty—about 2600 BC) is the earliest major stone structure in Egypt. For a structure about 4,500 years old, it and its adjacent temple, are in remarkably good shape.

We also visited the underground tomb or Mastaba of Ptah Hotep (about 2400 BC) with its spectacular carvings and paintings. On the way back toward Cairo we stopped at a rug weaving school to watch the weavers, mostly children from about 8 to about 16 years of age, learning the process and turning out rugs for sale.

From there we continued on to Giza where the three largest pyramids and the Sphinx are. When I was in Egypt many years ago, there were few tourists around and I was alone in the Kings chamber of the Great Pyramid (except for the small sweeper of dust!) This time, it was one continuous line of people up to the pyramid, into the pyramid, up to the inside chambers and then back down again. With this many people around it was impossible to even try to detect any subtle energies that might be present.

DK says as I write these notes:

"This was of no consequence. All that needed to happen, happened the first time so this visit to this structure was just for pleasure."

We then continued to the Sphinx. On my last visit I walked all around the Sphinx and even between its paws. This time there were high walls around it and you couldn't get within 100 feet of it. Too bad. It was wonderful to be able to touch it and walk completely around it.

I didn't bother to go to the pyramid of Chephren, the second largest pyramid on the plateau, this time. When I was there the first time I wandered into it and, after going down deep within it, was startled to see a room full of electronic equipment and an American physicist from the University of California. It turned out that they were running a cosmic ray absorption test (over many months) to see if there were any more chambers in the middle of the structure. Several years later I read in a journal that they hadn't found any.

The second day we went to a very old Jewish synagogue in Cairo where there is a large altar over the spot where it is believed that Moses was found in the bull rushes. Then on to another very old structure called St. Sargius church where it is believed that the Holy family stayed during their flight to Egypt. Obviously there wasn't a church there at that time, but this church is said to be the oldest in Egypt and it was supposedly built over the spot where this occured. In a little booklet put out by this church there is a wonderful writeup comparing the beliefs of the Western and Greek Christian churches, to that of the Christian church of the Copts, the Ethiopians, Armenians and Syrians. In one paragraph it says "The controversy (between the two Christian religions) is only a matter of wording. No doubt the belief of the Coptic Church is the correct and true one." Aren't each one of us so like that—believing that we are the right ones, no matter about what. There doesn't seem to be any indication of exactly when this church was built except some where between 296 AD and 859 AD.

The next morning we were off to the world famous Egyptian Museum. I had spent several happy hours here in my last trip, even hiring a guide to be sure I didn't miss anything. This time I had a number of things I specifically wanted to study, so it wasn't difficult to spend another few hours at this wonderful spot. I've been to museums in many cities that contain Egyptian antiquities, but I've never felt energy from any object in any of them—with the possible exception of the Egyptian section of the Metropolitan Museum in New York City. There, on a visit several years later, **DK** told me to sit in a particular spot between several statues and meditate for several minutes. Even then I didn't feel much energy, but at least I felt something.

That evening we took the train to Luxor. What a wonderful train ride. Although it was night when we left Cairo, we had two hours of daylight the next morning before reaching our destination. As we rode along the Nile in the morning, we could watch the farmers tending their crops, pumping water, and doing their chores. It seemed to be just as it must have been three to four thousand years ago. Most of the work is still done by hand or by animals. We saw almost no modern equipment anywhere—except for an occasional truck or bus along a roadway.

The town of Luxor is the center for visitors to Upper Egypt with the great temples of Karnak and the huge Temple of Luxor very nearby. Just across the Nile on the setting sun side are the Valley of the Kings and the Valley of the Queens where so many tombs are located.

We started with a boat ride across the Nile to the Valley of the Kings, visiting the tombs of Ramesses II, Tutankhamun, and later the great Temple of Queen Hatshepsut. On the way back we stopped at the Great Mortuary temple built by Ramesses II called the Ramesseum, and at the Colossi of Memnon, those huge seated statues now standing alone because the stone from their surrounding temple was taken to be used for other buildings.

The next day we visited the temples of Karnak and the Great Temple of Luxor. It was all very special and fascinating and I wouldn't have missed it for anything, but I was disappointed to not feel energy anywhere.

We left the next day for Cairo and to catch our bus to the Holy Land.

We crossed the Suez Canal just north of Ismailia after spending the night there. Crossing the Sinai Desert on the northern most route (Highway 55) we occasionally caught glimpses of an oasis, disabled tanks still remaining from the Six Day War, and a look now and then at the Mediterranean Sea.

Security is very tight at the Israel border just south of Gaza and we spent well over an hour there with luggage inspection and personal interviews as to why we wanted to go to Israel. Driving through the Gaza strip, after finally clearing customs, we would occasionally hear thumps on the bus as rocks were thrown at it. However, the most interesting thing is the cultivation of the fields. All across the Sinai there are very few cultivated fields—just an occasional small one or two near an oasis. Other than this there is just sand. From the Israel border on, however, the land is in almost total cultivation.

We arrived in Tel Aviv in the afternoon. The following morning we drove to Old Jaffa, a settlement called Joppa in the Bible, and in existence from about 3000 BC. It is now well restored and lived in.

We continued north, soon reaching Caeserea, just a few

miles north of Tel Aviv and right on the coast. This is a partially restored settlement begun in the 4th century BC. Most of the buildings here were built for Herod and are now in the process of restoration.

Turning inland toward the Sea of Galilee, I was again struck by the cultivation of the fields almost everywhere. As we approached the ancient town of Capharnaum (also spelled Capernaum and Kapernaum) on the shore of the Sea of Galilee, we drove past the hill were it is believed that Christ gave the Sermon on the Mount. This town is one of the holy sites in Israel. It is believed to be the place where Christ met Peter and asked him to become "a fisher of men," and near where HE walked on water. It also contains ruins of what is believed to be Peter's house and a late fourth century AD synagogue which is believed to be built on the site of "the synagogue of Jesus." A wonderful place to visit—full of history and feelings of peace and quiet and knowledge that some of the sacred history of the Earth took place here.

After wandering through the ruins we boarded a large boat and motored across the Sea to Tiberias on its west bank. Following lunch we drove down to the Jordan River where a special place has been set apart for baptisms, and where I collected water to give to friends to baptize their children with.

Then on to the hilltop town of Nazareth where Jesus spent his childhood. Churches are everywhere there but the huge Church of the Annunciation is very large, modern and beautiful. This is not a small town any more. I had mixed feelings here. Probably too many changes and too much growth to feel any particular energies.

On the way to Jerusalem we passed Mount Tabor, the believed site of Christ's transfiguration and stopped at the town of Jericho where the Tell of Old Jericho is. This site is believed by many to be the location of the oldest city on Earth, dating back to about 8000 BC. Just west of Jericho is a mountain, called the Mount of Temptation, where it is believed that Christ fasted for forty days after being baptized by John and where it is believed that he was then tempted by the devil.

As we drove up from Jericho to the hilltop where Jerusalem is located we passed through desert and into steep canyons, one containing the Monastery of St. George, precariously clinging to one side.

There is no place on Earth quite like Jerusalem. Covering the entire top of the hill, it is a very special place to be. In Hebrew its name is Yerushalayim or Dwelling of Peace. In Arabic its name is El-Quds or Holy. Discovery of flint tools and graves nearby indicate that man was living there in the Old Stone Age. In the time of Abraham (about 1800 BC), the town was called Salem, meaning "peace." The Temple of David and Solomon was here. Christ was crucified and buried here. Mohammed "ascended to heaven" here. Thus the site is revered by the three monotheistic religions of Judaism, Christianity and Islam.

We spent several days in and around Jerusalem, partly with tours and partly on our own. I wanted to fly to Saint Catherine's Monastery in the Sinai where it is believed that Moses watered the flocks of his father-in-law, and where he saw the burning bush. In back of this monastery is Gebel Musa (the Mount of Moses) on which Moses is believed to have been given the Tablet of Commandments by God. However, since no one else seemed interested in going, the trip was cancelled. Another visit that I apparently shouldn't make.

The trips to the three sacred sites in Jerusalem turned out to be phenomenal—and totally unexpected. The first stop was the Western (formerly the Wailing) Wall. The Wall wasn't too crowded at this time and there was no problem in walking up to it. Now what? Looking around I saw that some were just standing there praying, others had their foreheads against it, some praying silently, others out loud. I suddenly liked the idea of putting my forehead—the site of the third eye or the 6th chakra—against it and allowing the wall to do its thing. What an immediate effect! I don't remember feeling any specific energy transfer, or getting any messages from it, but did the tears start to flow! They flowed on and on. I have no idea how long I was there, but the tears flowed the whole time. I finally pulled myself away and slowly left that totally unexpected place of power with the knowledge that it will again become a place for universal prayer—not just for those who consider themselves Jewish.

The next stop was the Church of the Holy Sepulcher which is believed to be over the places where Christ was both crucified and buried. As I reached the place of crucifixion, I stepped out of line and just stood there, trying to feel what had happened either here—or at least somewhere near here, almost two thousand years ago. Again the tears started to flow, and again they continued until I finally moved away. This time I also felt sorrow, although not for The Christ since his end was ordained and necessary. Rather, I felt sorrow for all of the millions of additional deaths that have taken place because of His death.

As I write these notes, **DK** says:

"The Christ was sent to be a philosopher and teacher, trying to teach others some of the things he had learned. There was no need for these additional deaths. All would have happened as foretold if more patience and wisdom had been exercised by all those involved. But man is not yet a patient being. Many more deaths will occur over religion before mankind finally reaches the stage where all can go their own way, and believe as they wish, instead of trying to force others to believe as they do."

At the place of His tomb I visited the back of it, where there was only a priest and me, instead of the front entrance with its long line of people. The result was the same as at the place of crucifixion—suddenly lots of tears. But this time there was not so much sadness. Rather I felt a combination of love, and hope, and a knowledge that all is slowly working out and that all was not in vain.

The fourth sacred stop was to The Dome of the Rock, the third most important Islamic shrine after Mecca and Medina. This shrine is located on the spot where it is believed that Mohammed ascended to heaven, then returned to Mecca. The Jews and the Moslems also believe that it was on this place that Abraham was about to sacrifice Isaac. Again, I had no idea what to expect here or even what was inside of the Dome. After taking off my shoes and leaving the camera with a friend outside as requested, I slowly proceeded into this huge structure. As I walked around the inside wall I noticed an object in the middle. As I walked closer, I could see a large corner of rock extending up through the floor. Finally, on the side farthest from the entry door, there were stairs going down into the rock where there was some sort of a cave. I later found out that this cave is called "Bir el Arwah" or "Fountain of Souls" and it is believed that this cave is where souls of the dead gather to pray.

After going down the steps and into the small cave I again stepped aside from the line of people into a little corner and, touching the cave walls, closed my eyes. For the fourth time that morning tears started to flow. But here there was no unhappiness—only a calm, gentle flow of energy and I knew that the cave was just as holy a spot as the other three and here, one can:

"Go to quiet and rebuild one's Soul."

(Again **DK** has taken over to state this.) I stayed in there for perhaps fifteen minutes before slowly going back outside to the bright sunlight.

After my unexpected and very powerful feelings at each of these sacred sites, the rest of the trip was of less importance. However, it was still a joy to walk the Via Delorosa (the path that Christ took on his way to crucifixion), to go to Bethlehem (now a suburb of Jerusalem), to walk into the room where the Last Supper may have been held, to walk in Gethsemane, to go down into the Church of the Assumption, and to the Mount of Olives.

On the day I had planned to go to Saint Catherine's I went instead to Massada with stop overs on the Dead Sea and at Qumrun where the Dead Sea Scrolls were found.

All in all, a trip never to be forgotten.

CHAPTER 7

TRAVEL: EASTER ISLAND

I had wanted to go to Easter Island for years, but no one seemed to know how to get there. Every travel agent I contacted showed no interest in tracking down the route and airlines involved. I finally did the necessary research myself and found, as usual, that it was no big deal. You simply fly down to Santiago, Chile and then catch the flight that stops at Easter Island on the way to Tahiti.

Then a strange thing happened. The company I was working for had an off-site "get away" management meeting and my roommate turned out to be someone interested in the Ouija Board. I had always thought this was a child's game, not a serious tool. But when he suggested that we try it one evening, since I was a professional experimenter, I agreed.

At first we got nothing from it, just a bunch of letters, but the number 3 kept appearing and my roommate said he wondered if we needed three people to "run" it this time? Just then someone knocked on the door! He had come for some reason that I can't now remember, and also thought the Ouija was a bunch of nonsense, but agreed to try it with us. With the three of us touching the planchette, all of a sudden, the board came to life. What follows is an approximate recording of what followed. It is approximate because I couldn't write fast enough to keep up with it, sometimes not getting the full question. I have, therefore, had to use my memory to some extent on this part. The answers, since they were written down as they occurred, are exact.

"We would like to ask you some questions about H. King."

(These questions were mostly asked by the board owner. I hadn't any idea what to do or ask. The questions were asked verbally. I then wrote down the answers on a piece of paper as they were spelled out—one letter at a time—by the board. Because there is no punctuation, and all the letters run together, it is often quite a challenge to make sense of the results.)

Is his spiritual guide there? YES
Are you a good or a bad guide?   GOOD
What is your name?   ARCMINUS
Do you have anything to say to him?
TRAVEL EASTER ISLAND
(There had been no mention of Easter Island before this
    in this room.)
Concerning what? SEA TRAVEL
From where?   ATLANTIS
About what?   FINDING SPECIAL ARTIFACTS
How will he find it?   TRY HARD
What will he find? NOT KNOWN TO MAN
Where will it be?   IN SEA
Near the shore?   NEAR SHORE
What will it look like?   METALLIC OBJECT
Will it be silvery? NO
Will it be copper? INDIUM
From another world?   YES
What will it look like?   POINTED
How will I see it? IT WILL BE DIFFICULT TO SEE
Is it a weapon?   NO
How will I find it? U WILL FEEL IT

Will there be water on it? NO
Will it be at high or low tide?   LOW TIDE
Will I find it the first day? NO
Will I find it the second day?   2nd SUNDAY
What is it? IT IS OF THE SUN
How big is it?   YOU CAN CARRY IT
Where is it from? ATLANTIS
Is it from this dimension? NO, OTHER DIMENSION
What should I do with it? KEEP SAFE
How will I find it? FEEL WITH FEET
How will I know when I have found it?
      FEET WILL HURT
Should I show it to others? NO KEEP TO SELF
How will I know when I have found it?   WILL KNOW
Will it be near a rock?
(Then followed a detailed description of the location
      giving rock shape, roads nearby, etc.)
How did it get there?   ACCIDENT
Accident from the sun?   YES
From a spacecraft? NO
From where?   ATLANTIS
Is it from the moon?   MANY MOONS
What is it used for? TRAVEL
Can I use it for anything?
      INVESTIGATION OF TRAVEL
Was this used to investigate travel? YES
What kind of travel?   SUN TRAVEL
Is it time or space travel? TIME TRAVEL
Will I know how to use it? IN TIME
Will it be on Earth as we know it today?   NO
Do you have a message for M—? BE HAPPY
Do you have a message for N—? TOUCH SPIRIT
(These were the other two participants)

79

I think we all were in shock after this experience. I couldn't ever have imagined such an intelligent conversation! But I at least now knew that I should go to Easter Island and that I should be there for at least two Sundays. As I looked back over this conversation, it is fairly obvious that our questions weren't the best—but we had no time to prepare for it. It just happened and we had to react as best we could.

With this data in mind I went ahead and made the necessary reservations, being sure that I would be on the island for two Sundays—actually staying on the island for 1 and 1/2 weeks.

I hoped to be able to totally walk around the island, which would take about three days, during this stay. I took a tent and sleeping bag, as well as provisions, and spent several weeks, before I left, hiking in my neighborhood with the pack to be sure I would be in shape.

I left on October 5, 1987 for New York City and later that evening on LanChile for Santiago, Chile. It was an uneventful, 12 hour flight, although sunrise over the Andes was spectacular. I had a day in Santiago before the flight to Easter Island (they only fly there twice a week) and spent it just wandering around that interesting city.

Easter Island is said to be the most remote inhabited island on Earth and I can believe it. We flew for more than four hours over the Pacific Ocean without seeing land of any kind. On arriving, the first thing I needed was a place to stay since I had no reservations. As we entered the airport there were several women standing near the door, looking for customers for their penciones or small hotels. I had gotten the name of one particular pencione from a travel book, and since the person for this place was there I was all set. She took me to the converted home—a distance of perhaps three miles—by old car. After leaving my backpack there, and carefully noting exactly were we were, since her house was quite a distance back from the dirt road and couldn't be seen from it, I left for the short walk to the coast.

I had obtained a map of the island before arriving and had decided generally where this item that I was supposed to find might be. As I headed for the coast—a distance of about 1/2 mile—I could see some of the huge famous carved figures (called moai) off in the distance. They became my first stop. All the moai—dozens of them—had been toppled from their carefully prepared bases some 100 to 300 years ago. From about 1955 on, there have been attempts to restore some of them to their original splendor. They have done this with great success, except for one area on the southeast part of the island where one entire, restored group was knocked down again by a recent tidal wave!

When you walk up to a group of restored moai on their base, the feeling is overpowering. These figures are typically from 20 to 30 feet tall (as tall as a two story building) and with several of them side by side you can almost feel the energy that must have been expended to first carve, then transport, and finally erect them entirely by hand. By the way, each moai is different. Their face, ears, chest, backs and hands all look about the same until you see several side by side. Then you begin to pick out significant differences and begin to realize that these are depictions of individuals, not just repeating figures of a god.

As I walked along the coastline towards the only town on the island, Hanga Roa, about a mile or two away, I thought I saw two or three places that might fit my instructions in finding this antiquity—whatever it was. The walk itself was delightful. This is a totally volcanic island, roughly triangular in shape (about 10 to 20 miles per side) with a large, extinct volcano at each corner and about twelve more, mostly smaller, volcanoes scattered within the resulting triangle. One of these in particular, Rano Raraku, is the "birthing area" where most of the statues were carved out of the volcanic rock. There are still dozens or perhaps even hundreds of the moai here in this extinct volcano—still in their "womb"—that were in the process of being carved when all work on them suddenly stopped. One of these is about 60 feet tall! Many others were completed and in the process of being moved down the mountain towards the coast when abandoned.

Hanga Roa is the only town on the island. It is right on the coast, with a very small harbor where small boats can come in to unload. There are about 1600 Rapanui, as they call themselves, and another 1000 or so continentales or Chilean government employees living there. On my second evening there I walked into town to meet a group of people from Earth Watch who were there on an archeological dig. On the way there, I happened to look up at the sky. I have never seen a night sky so beautiful. The sky was just ablaze with stars— stars I had never seen before. Absolutely spectacular!

On my second day there I wandered along most of the west coast of the island and the third day along most of the south coast, looking for that telltale rock shape and nearby roads and just enjoying the wonderful and unusual scenery. Oh, is it windy there! What a wonderful place for windmills to generate power. Everywhere I went, that was near the coast, there was a strong, continuous wind.

The history of the Easter Island peoples is strange and in most cases tragic. The first settlers are believed to have arrived there between 100 and 500 AD. These settlers carried a round stone about a foot in diameter which is supposed to still be on what is believed to be their landing beach. This stone is called "the navel of the world." The whole island itself is also called "the navel of the world" (Te Pito o Te Henua). Most believe that these explorers came from Eastern Polynesia, although a small group of archaeologists believe that they came from Peru, because the walls near some of the moai are almost identical in construction to many Peruvian walls.

Because much of their history is lost it is not known for sure how they developed over the next 1000 years or so. It is thought that there developed a two-tiered society, the "long ears" and the "short ears" with the long ears in control. The long ears made the short ears carve the moai, among other things. The short ears finally rebelled (probably in the 1600s) and killed all but one of the long ears (hence the sudden cessation of carving and moving of the moai.)

Exploring and trading vessels began arriving in the 1700's, occasionally killing some Rapanui, bringing disease and taking slaves. In 1862, slavers took over 1000 to work in Peru. Included in this group was the last king and the entire learned class. Eventually 15 surviving islanders from this large group were allowed to return, bringing back more disease with them. Shortly after 1865, the entire island was converted into a sheep ranch and many of the remaining islanders were forcibly sent to Tahiti. Returnees from Tahiti brought back leprosy. By 1870 the population was down to 110. None of these knew their history or could read their very special and unusual language carved on wooden boards called "rongo rongo." The island continued as a sheep ranch until 1953, with the Rapanui restricted to just a tiny area of their island. Surely this is one of the sadder tales of human cruelty. Incidentally, the guide another traveler and I hired for one day to show us the island was a "leftover" from the sheep ranch days, having been one of the British overseers.

Now I began the work of finding the object—if there was such a thing—in earnest, while at the same time enjoying this wonderful and very special place. The particular rock shape I was looking for was turning out to be something of a problem. Volcanic rocks tend to have strange shapes which should be recognizable. But this is a totally volcanic island and there are thousands of large, strange shaped rocks all along the coast. By eliminating areas that weren't near the particular roads mentioned in the reading, I succeeded in narrowing down the possible number of sites to about five, with one prime suspect. I then needed to find out what the schedule of the tides was since "it" should be found at low tide. This I found at the local Hydrographic office.

How do you find something that is 1) "difficult to see" 2) would be "felt with the feet" and 3) you would know you had found it when "your feet hurt"? I divided up the likely areas and started looking at each in greater detail, at low tide, wandering around them in bare feet—a difficult task because volcanic rock can be very sharp. I wasn't sure exactly what I was looking for, and I'm sure I looked like a fool doing it with my pants rolled up to the knees as I dug my toes in the wet sand. Since low tide only occurs twice a day, for perhaps an hour or less each time, the hunt was severly restricted. I would look during low tide and wander the island the rest of the day. By the time the 2nd Sunday rolled around I knew the coastline of that island like a native, and must have walked around 100 or more likely rocks in bare feet at low tide!

You probably think I was stupid for working at it so carefully and systematically. But first, I didn't want to take a chance of not finding "it," if I possibly could. And second, what a wonderful way to get to know a place. Just wandering around would never have given me the insight into the people and the geology, that I got by this intense scrutiny.

That second Sunday, since I hadn't found anything yet, I decided to walk the entire coastline where I thought it might be—at least 8 miles of very rugged beach and coastline with few paths anywhere. No luck. Not even a twinge of pain, except when I stepped on something sharp accidentally. I spent the next day (My last full day there) just soaking up the atmosphere. I hadn't felt anything special anywhere here, other than when looking up at the moai. I certainly knew this island though! Far better than I had ever expected. I had explored caves; I had spent a day and a half with Earth Watch on an archeological dig; I had hiked up two of the three large volcanoes and had explored their petroglyphs and ancient, rebuilt long houses. I knew miles of its coastline better than the back of my hand and had met many interesting people. What more could you ask for?

On the return trip to the U.S., I enjoyed another day in Santiago before heading home. About three weeks later we held another Ouija session to try to find out why my search hadn't been successful. We didn't get as clear a transmission as last time, possibly because we didn't have the same three people. We had two, of the original three, however. We got another guide, named "Alenmama," who said "English no good". It went approximately as follows:

Why didn't I find the object? THOUGHT YOU HAD
    ALREADY OPENED 3RD EYE
Should I go back when this occurs?
    GO THRU TIME NO BODY NOT
    NECESSARY LEAVE IT I CHING
    HK STUDY 3 GO THRU CLOSED
    DOOR TRAVEL NO BODY STUDY
    CRYSTAL FIND WHAT IS LOST
    NOT TO FEAR FROM BEYOND
    HK LEARN I CHING 30

As you can see this was pretty garbled, and was answers to several questions, but I got the feeling that I should not go back until I had opened the third eye and then should not go back physically, but by spirit or soul travel! After this session I purchased several translations of the I Ching, and looked up chapters 3 and 30. I couldn't find anything specific in these that might help my search but enjoyed the book very much.

Let's now ask **DK** for his comments about this trip (November,1991):

"This was an exceptional trip for you even though you didn't think you found what you were looking for. We often give students tasks to do and the point is not to find what they were sent for but for them to demonstrate their ability in trying to carry out the task. The end point is unimportant. You expended exceptional effort in trying to find this object—and you actually did find it, although you didn't recognize it. There is no need for you to go back there now since you will be able to time travel without the use of any external device."

Since we have already talked about the Ouija Board this might be a good time to mention a few more encounters I had with it some time later. I should note, however, that since my direct contacts with **DK** started, in 1989, I can no longer use the Ouija Board. Nothing happens anymore.

In all cases we found that there had to be three or more people using it at one time. I also want to strongly recommend that it NOT be used by children—only by mature (mentally as well as physically) adults. It can be a dangerous device if not used carefully. For instance, after completing one session (by the guide saying "that is all for now" or something like that) one of our users tried to ask more questions. We all suddenly felt evil coming out through it. We immediately upset the board and mentally sent it Love energy, and further flushed out our minds with Light and Love energies). The Board should not be used after such an occurrence for at least 24 hours and preferably longer, but this occurrence should not have been allowed to happen in the first place. When it says "stop" or "we are through," or whatever—stop using it!

In any case, what follows are the results of two other sessions that I found records of in my files:

May 7, 1988
Who are we speaking to? TIAMET
Are you anyone's guide? C—(One of the participants)
Where is she from (In a past incarnation?) LUXOR
Are you from a star? ALL ARE
Which star? KARMA PROHIBITS
Do you have a message for C— STOP NEGATIVITY.
   OPEN UP. LET
   KARMA FLOW. (YOU) MUST BE
   EARTH BOUND. DEPENDS ON HER
   FACING CHALLENGE OF EARTH.
What is her mission on Earth? KARMA.
   ACCEPTING HOMO SAPIENS.
   SHE IS NEEDED TO OPEN UP OTHERS
   TO WHAT SHE KNOWS.
What does she know? (THAT) OTHER
   REALITIES EXIST.
   SHE FEELS TRUTH.
Should she write about this? WAIT UNTIL SHE IS 38.
Should HK write a book? WHEN HE IS 61. (I was 62 when I actually started this book although I had been thinking about it for about a year.)
   HK KNOWS ENOUGH NOW.
   TY TOGETHER TRIPS.
   WHAT DID HK LEARN?

Is there a better way to use this board?
    AUTOMATIC WRITING,
    TRANCE CHANNEL
How?   ALL CAN DO. CLC 12
What is the significance of CLC12?
    CFR. ALL CAN BELIEVE. KEY
    (IS) ALL TO BELIEVE.
Is channeling dangerous? EVERYTHING
    DANGEROUS OR
    NOTHING DANGEROUS. RELATIVE.
What does the number 888 mean? NYC 88
    1988 POWER SPOT. DATE IS
    SIGNIFICANT.
Should HK go to NYC on that date? DEFINITELY
    YES. MEDITATE. MEET
    CHANNEL. 152A SHORE DRIVE
    ANSWER.

Because of this data on August 8, 1988 I took a day off from work and flew from Boston to New York City. Once there, I went to the city library on Fifth Ave. to try to find a Shore Drive. There was only one that I could find listed in all the maps I looked at and it was in the Bronx. After a two hour additional journey, first on the subway, then on a bus, then a several block walk, I arrived at Shore Drive. I had no idea what I would find or what I would say once I got there, but what the heck. This was just another strange adventure.

Once there I began walking up Shore Drive. Unfortunately this was not a regular street. It was broken up into many, short, unconnected pieces and I couldn't find a number 152A. I found a mailman to ask, and two people I asked gave me rides in their cars trying to find such a place but no luck. There wasn't such a number. After about two hours of searching for this address I gave up. It then took another two hours or so to get back to Manhattan. I bought detailed maps of all the other boroughs in case they might be newer than the maps in the library. I had no luck in finding such a street name anywhere else, so after six hours in New York City I caught the next shuttle to Boston and then home to New Hampshire, thoroughly discouraged.

On the next Ouija session about four weeks later I asked the board why I hadn't found this place. The answer was terse: **NEEDED ENERGY 8888. DID FIND. NOW CALL**

Apparently I had needed more energy to continue with my studies, and this method was used to get me to New York City where I could get that energy. The fact that there was no 152A Shore Drive was unimportant. If I had found such an address I wouldn't have stayed there long enough so I had to be given an address that didn't exist so it would take me a long time to search for it!

Ouija session on Sept. 5, 1988:
Who are we speaking to?   NDAD CAMELIA
Is Camelia your name?   YES
Are you a good spirit?   YES
(Apparently all answers MUST be truthful so this is a good question to start out with.)

    HK. YC CHANNEL M.LURIA TELEPHONE
    NUMBER——— CALL 9 12 88
What area code?   617
What town?   ——— (A town in Massachusetts)
Why couldn't HK find 152A Shore Drive?
    NEEDED ENERGY 8888
    DID FIND NOW CALL
(Note: I called the number given, on that date, as directed. This turned out to be a very strange and exciting telephone call.

89

The results are reported in Chapter 9.)

Any other messages?

Who is there now?   HECTOR

Are you a good spirit?   YES

Are you a spirit guide of anyone here?   NO

Any messages for anyone here?   DNOQ YES NAME

Is that your last name Hector?   RAYNONDNOQ

What time period are you from?   INCA

Who made the Nazca Lines?   STAR PEOPLE

What star were they from?   DO NOT KNOW

When did they draw them?   BEFORE MY BIRTH

When were you born?   12 AD

I though the Incas came in after 800 AD?

WE ARE OLD CIVILIZATION

What did you do there?   MASON

Why are you talking to us?   WATCHED HK

ON TRIP. MAYAN(trip?)

Are Mayans also an old civilization?   AZTEC ALSO

What about the Olmecs?   DO NOT THEM KNOW

What were the Nazca Lines used for?   SPIRITUAL

HEALING AND TRAVEL OF SOUL

OF LEARNED

How did the star people use them?   TEACH TO FIND

Find what?   US(E) MAP A DRAWING OF LOCATION

(HK Note: Does this mean the lines are a map locating
their star?)

Can we use the lines to find directions?

ART OF USE LOST. TIME AND
DIMENSION TRAVEL. CARLOS
KASENATA CLOSE. HE IS ON TRACK
BUT NOT THERE YET. HE HAS NOT
APPLIED KNOWLEDGE TO LINES.
SHOULD.

Is it possible to get music on the Ouija? ASK MUSICIAN.
ME HECTOR LIKE TO DRAW

(HK note: In our next session M——, one of the participants in this session, modified a ballpoint pen to fit on the planchette and Hector drew some wonderful, simple line pictures—very similar to some of Picasso's line drawings!)

The Ouija can be very critical of someone as well as helpful. In the next statements from this September session Hector said the following to one of the people with me on the Board:

LOOK WITHIN. LAZY. ONCE NOT ENOUGH. LAZY. EASY WAY NO GOOD. WORK FOR IT. STOP LAZY. U DO NOT LISTEN. TOO MUCH BEER TALK. ACTION ACTION.

I didn't record the date of the following Ouija transmission or the question asked. However, I did write down this answer to a question so I could think more about it:

STUDY CRYSTALS TO LEARN TIME
TRAVEL THROUGH LIGHT. PLAIDES
SECRET.

CHAPTER 8

TRAVEL: PERU/ SHAMAN

I learned about this trip while leafing through a magazine I seldom looked at. I just happened to pick up this particular copy. I immediately wrote for information about the trip and then quickly signed up for it. How could one resist a trip that promises "A voyage of personal and planetary transformation, where we re-enact the journey taken by shamans to acquire spiritual knowledge, discover personal power, and become caretakers of the Earth." The brochure went on to say: "This is an intensive experiential journey that will take participants through the four points of the medicine wheel: To erase one's personal history in the South; to lose the fear of death in the West; to meet the Great Spirit in the North; and to discover one's power and visionary gifts in the East." (From a brochure by the Four Winds Foundation). Everything I always wanted to know—but didn't know whom to ask!

While I don't think they delivered all of this, they came closer to it than I believed possible. As with my second trip to India, this second trip to Peru proved to be much more powerful than my first trip. Perhaps it is necessary to come back a second time to sacred sites to achieve their full benefit. Perhaps I was just more developed by the time a second trip seemed worthwhile. Perhaps now was just the time for it. Or it may have been some of all of these.

April, 1988.

A few of us met at the airport in Miami before the flight to Peru. We didn't have any tags on, but I guess one nut can spot another because, by the time we were ready to get on the plane, four or five of us going on the journey where already talking together. All of the group met together for the first time at our hotel in Lima. There were about 17 of us from all over the United States, and I was surprised at their backgrounds. Two were PhD educators, one was a practicing PhD or DSc clinical psychologist. Most were college graduates. I seemed to be the only research scientist in the group.

This was the first time in twenty years of work that I had been with others who were also explorers of the unknown. How nice it was to learn that I wasn't all alone in this search! To be able to make comments and exchange ideas and talk of past experiences with others was wonderful.

The next morning, after a long bus and then a short boat ride, our first stop was at The Tree of Life or The Candelabra at Paracas Bay. The government of Peru forbids anyone to stop at this site because it is in sand and can be easily damaged. Many of the sites we were to visit were similarly protected. However, because we were traveling and working with a Peruvian Shaman—don Edwardo Calderon—we had special permission from the government to visit them. At one such site, The Nazca Lines, we invited the Peruvian Government's Head of Archeology for the region to conduct the ancient ceremony with us. His comment was "No thanks. I conducted it with your group last year and I'm still trying to recover from it!"

No one knows how old this figure outside Paracas Bay is because there are no artifacts with which to date it—just this enormous carving, about 600 feet long, in the sand of a steep hill, right on the Pacific Ocean. What a strange place for it, since it can only be seen from a boat or aircraft! The only reason it still exists is because there is essentially no rain there—ever! And it is difficult to get to. You have to wade through fairly high surf to get from the boat to the shore (there is no landing dock or wharf). Then you must hike a mile or more up to it through loose sand—no easy task. This figure may be several thousand years old or no more that two or three hundred, but it is awe inspiring to see, even from a long distance off in a boat.

The ceremony we conducted there consisted primarily of a meditation, lead by don Edwardo and his apprentice. Perhaps because there were so many of us meditating together at a powerful place I had a general feeling of energy there but nothing specific. I do remember during the meditation (with my eyes closed) of "seeing" blackness and then a pattern of many purple or lavender spots being superimposed on the blackness. These square spots remained for several minutes. This was unusual for me because I very seldom "see" color in my meditation or, for that matter, anything at all.

Our second stop was at the town of Nazca in southern Peru to work on, and with, the Nazca Lines. These lines are typically very long and very straight (often miles long) interspersed with outlines of many, very large figures of animals, insects, birds, a human-like figure, and flowers. No one knows for sure what these lines are for, although recent (1991) data by a new archeologist, working with Maria Reiche (an archaeologist who has worked on these lines for about forty years) and a computer, suggests they (and the symbols associated with the lines) point to particular stars about 2000 years ago. They are believed to have been drawn between about 500 BC and 100 AD but no one really knows for sure.

DK says:

"The Ouija session discussing them in the previous chapter of this book gives more accurate information about

them, although both are generally correct. They are a map of the stars and will guide you if you know how to use them.

"These particular figures were drawn by a people from distant stars who came to Earth to experience and absorb a particular type of Earth energy which they needed for their continued growth. Because they were here for many generations, the figures were placed there to teach and guide future generations back to their home star system. This group was here many, many thousands of years ago, not about 2000 years ago as suggested."

To the shaman, Nazca is the place one comes to meet one's power animals. Our work with the lines was to begin the night after our arrival, so we flew over the lines in the morning (the only way you can really see them), and learned more about shamanism and our ceremony in the afternoon. We also found and carved our "history stick" which was to contain those items of our past history which we wanted to shed.

We would be working with one of the many Nazca figures, "The Spiral" and the connected "Needle and Thread" which apparently were specifically intended for the use to which we put them. The "Needle and Thread" was particularly interesting because the thread wove back and forth across the needle seven times (once for each chakra?).

This ceremony was designed to work with the medicine wheel's South and was intended to erase one's personal history, so one could move forward into a new life unhindered. The ceremony began when full darkness arrived. As part of the ceremony, after the shaman had cleansed and purified the area and the participants and called in the necessary energies, we were each given purification fluids which will be described later. A person, with history stick in hand, is led to, and begins walking into, the spiral. On entry to the spiral a second person with a large sacred knife slashes down just in back of you to symbolically cut off any problem energy that may be following or trailing from you. On reaching the center of the spiral you thrust the stick into the ground with great force and an explosive shout, releasing any problem energies you may have contained within you. You then walk back out of the spiral purified.

There is a ceremony before you enter the spiral to cleanse yourself and make sure that you are performing it for spiritual reasons. A part of that ceremony includes the pouring of the contents of a small clam shell full of a mixture of alcohol with tobacco juice dissolved in it down your nose. I say "down" because your head is tipped back so the mixture can run down the inside of the nose. This feels even worse than it sounds. Some of the mixture runs down your face and into your mouth, or down your chin and onto your neck and clothes. The rest runs through the nose, and down your throat. It tastes and smells awful, as well as causing a lot of coughing, snorting and sneezing. Everyone got some of it down, however.

Tobacco is, of course, one of the great purifiers in shamanism. However, it is usually smoked by the shaman and the smoke is wafted over your body to spiritually cleanse it. Drinking it may give you a greater effect, but it sure is awful to taste. And having it run down your nose and throat and chin is not very pleasant. Needless to say, the effect of the alcohol and tobacco can be very rapid and powerful because the nose has many blood vessels and is obviously very close to the brain. Fortunately only a small amount of this stuff was absorbed, the rest running down the face or being expelled in coughing and sneezing.

Normally I wouldn't have taken any compound of any kind, since I have never smoked or taken drugs or any alcohol (other than perhaps a small sip of wine once a year or so) or even coffee or tea. (I do enjoy chocolate, however.) I don't even take aspirin or cold pills unless I really feel low. In this case, however, on the last use of the Ouija Board before going on this trip, in answer to my question, " Any questions about Peru?" It suddenly spelled out:

DRUG
Are you saying that I should take no drug?
NO. NEED DRUG
For what?
TO LEARN, OPEN SOUL. SEE OWL HORUS HK
SPIRIT GOD
Is an owl my spirit animal?
YES ALWAYS
Can I Open the third eye?
WITH CACTUS

The second potion taken, following the alcohol/tobacco mix, was a special fluid prepared by the shaman and made from the San Pedro cactus. Proportions of ingredients for this mix must be quite exact, and prepared and used with great care. The San Pedro cactus is considered one of the most, if not the most hallucinogenic of all plants. In addition to this solution, don Edwardo also added a small amount of a potion made from the Sacred Datura or Jimson Weed, another hallucinogenic but even more dangerous plant. (It might be interesting to note here that this same Sacred Datura grows wild around my new Arizona home, growing within a few feet of the house.)

With proper ceremony, a small amount of this combined mixture (perhaps a tablespoon full) was given to each of us. Within minutes of taking this second compound my legs began to feel rubbery, and in a few more minutes I was unconscious. I was the only one to do so, I was later told. All the others completed the ceremony, going through the spiral and then sat and meditated or walked down the needle and thread, stopping at each crossing or chakra for further meditation. The ceremony started at about 10 PM and ended about 2 AM. Until I woke up the next morning—at my usual time of about 6 AM— I remember nothing, except when they tried to pick me up at 2 AM to carry me back to the bus, to return to the hotel. Then I remember begging them not to take me away from the beautiful, surrounding "lighted" rocks that were glowing with every color of the rainbow.

When I did wake up the next morning, fully clothed and on top of the bed where I had been dumped, I had no ill effects of the previous night—no headache, no tiredness, no memory (except of the glowing rocks), nothing. In fact, I felt so good that I decided to go for a walk around the small hotel where we were staying. There was only one other member of the group up—the PhD educator from New York City. I asked her how she was and she said she was looking for the lady's room. We were staying in a small, single level motel in the form of a figure eight with only about thirty rooms, and I had just passed a lady's room. I told her that while I couldn't remember where it was, if she would just wait there, I would go back and find it then come back to tell her where it was.

I found it a few minutes later and went back to tell her where it was, but when I found her I again couldn't remember the room's location. I went back again—and again—to find it, and each time when I got back to her I couldn't tell her where it was. This happened six times in quick succession! I never was able to tell her where it was. I don't know if she ever found it on her own or not. Apparently I had lost the ability to remember and integrate facts! What a thing to happen to a scientist whose whole life is based on doing just that! It turned out to be no problem, however, because within a few hours I could do it again.

A little later in this book, when I am talking directly to **DK**, he explains what happened there. At that time he asked me:

"What do you suppose questions do?"

I said "They make you think." He then answered:

"Yes, sometimes they make your mind break down, don't they? And that's helpful, isn't it? What happens when the mind breaks down?"

I answered "Then new channels are opened." He then replied:

"You've got it. You see, then you get to bridge from the new place to the old, don't you?"

The ceremony, the very powerful and ancient environment, and the drugs had worked together to force my mind to find millions of new channels for the thought process. I was, in effect, a totally new and different person and could now use the mind in different ways than it had ever been used before. (As I write this **DK** is concurring with this conclusion.) None of this was noticeable to me, however, until I started working with **DK** more directly, some time later. I didn't notice any greater or different mental abilities in my work, for instance. There was also no noticeable opening of the third eye. I didn't start seeing auras, for instance.

(Note: The drugs described here—as well as other sacred drugs—should NEVER be used by anyone except in the most carefully controlled conditions and with experts in complete control. They are VERY dangerous and in most cases will permanently HARM—not help—their taker!)

We left Nazca the following day for the long drive back to Lima for a flight into the Andes to the city of Cuzco, the largest and most important city in the entire Western Hemisphere when the Spanish first arrived.

I have heard that when the Spaniards first caught site of this city from the mountain passes surrounding it, they were almost blinded by the reflected light from the sun shining on the gold surfaces that were everywhere. There was more gold here than even the Spaniards could imagine. Temples covered and filled with gold. Monuments of it. Ritual baths of it. Unfortunately, after looting the city, they then proceeded to level nearly all of it and rebuilt it to suit themselves, essentially destroying a culture. However, this city, at about 11,000 feet elevation, almost the same as Leh in Ladakh, survived even this indignity. Today it is a thriving city of about 150,000 (and still without a single modern high rise building!). Its population is almost entirely Indian, with a few mestizo (a mix of Indian and Spanish).

I had not expected anything spiritual to happen here since I had been here just a few years before. But was I wrong. Apparently my continuing development had made me more sensitive to past life flows, because within five minutes of landing here, and while sitting in the Airport awaiting our bus to the city, the tears began to flow again and they continued for more than fifteen minutes! Talk about embarrassing! They just flowed on and on. Just before the bus arrived to take us to our hotel, they finally stopped and I got on the bus almost dry eyed.

As we started to drive through the city the tears started up again. This time they were so powerful that I had to ask the young lady sitting next to me (also a member of the group) if I could hold her hand for a moment. The feelings were so powerful that I simply had to touch a living, warm human. She must have seen what I was going through, because she allowed me to. The tears continued flowing all the way to our small, 200 year old hotel.

In a thought transmission I received almost a year later—on Jan 27, 1989 at 4 AM—I suddenly learned what these tears were all about. In a previous life one of the women that I was presently working with, and I, had been married, and had two children. We lived in Cuzco just prior to the time of the Spanish Conquest. The children and I were killed during a native uprising and my wife had then become a "Handmaiden to the gods," whatever that was. Were these tears in response to this past life and for the children and my wife?

As I write this **DK** is saying:

"Yes and no. The tears were for the wasted life that you led and for the life which your wife then had to lead because of your stupidity!"

The next day we visited the wonderful ruins at Sacsahuaman and conducted a cleansing ceremony at the ancient ritual baths at Tambomachay (called The Temple of the Waters). Here we washed in each of the three streams—with local natives watching. Immediately above these ruins we also began to work with our power animals for the first time, mimicking their movements and calling them to us. We then drove up to an ancient Inca fortress on the mountain side above Pisac where we conducted a late-night fire ceremony.

The following day we drove through the Andes and along the Urubamba River and Valley to the village and Inca fortifications at Olantatambo. This is a five hundred year old—or more (**DK** says actually more than a thousand years old!)—Inca village still in everyday use. Incidentally, the word Inca means "child of the sun" and originally was applied only to the ruler (Does this sound like the Egyptian Pharaoh Akhenaten? More on him later). This is the place where you really get to see Inca architecture. We saw some of their wonderful walls in Cuzco and Sacsahuaman but here, extending up the mountain, are walls, buildings and monuments. Wonderful things. You can't imagine fine stone work until you see Inca stone work. It puts all others to shame. Stones, with many sides and angles, meeting so precisely that a sheet of paper won't go in between them. Stones, not flat-sided, but cupped so one stone fits into another, not just on top of another. No mortar anywhere and still standing after very substantial earthquakes.

As I looked down on the Urubamba River flowing nearby I was startled to see that it was flowing in a straight line with stone banks on either sides. The Inca actually channeled this fierce river to prevent erosion and to permit irrigation! This is the one place where the Spanish were defeated militarily. This was done by purposely flooding this whole plain. The Inca had realized that the horses that the Spanish used so effectively couldn't operate in water. So they covered the whole plain with water by flooding it! This tactic stopped the Spanish advance for more than a year.

Another interesting remnant of this amazing civilization is their spectacular stone terraces—in many places going up the mountains for hundreds of feet, and extending over miles of very steep land. In one place we saw a large inverted pyramid built into the soil instead of going up from the soil. It is now believed that this was an experimental garden, each one foot or so step, going down into the large hole, being roughly equivalent to going down a thousand feet of elevation, (from a temperature standpoint). In this way the Inca could experiment with plants, finding which would grow in different areas on these very steep mountains.

The train going down the Urubamba River Canyon to Machu Picchu was an experience all by itself. The canyon is so steep in most places that a roadway would have been next to impossible to build. This single track railroad, just barely clinging to the steep mountains, was built just to take travelers to this ancient city in the clouds.

"Machu Picchu has been called the Inca City of Light and in ancient times could only be entered by persons who, through study and meditation, had reconciled themselves with death and understood the lessons of immortality." (This quote is from the Four Winds Foundation Brochure.) Here we were to discover the shamans' way of seeing, and to take part in a ritual to heal ourselves, and take the next step in our spiritual development.

What superlatives can one use to describe the first view of this sacred place? From the train stop all you see are very steep mountains and, every now and then, a piece of roadway snaking up to the top of one in particular. You only really see the city suddenly, once you get to the top (by small bus). I had thought that Darjeeling was spectacular. But Machu Picchu is even more so, because it is built to human scale. No huge single mountain across a large valley as in Darjeeling. Here you are surrounded by steep mountain peaks that are so close that you feel that you can almost reach out and touch them. Below you is the raging Urubamba River that you can walk down to in a few minutes. And everywhere there is tropical vegetation with some eighty varieties of orchids growing in the vicinity. And the city! Perfect in almost all respects, except for the straw roofs which had quickly deteriorated. A small city of terraces and monuments and buildings and grass walkways. The "city" covers just the hilltop between even higher and steeper peaks, but stone terraces to permit the growing of crops go both higher and lower than the buildings.

After spending a day and a night here, and conducting ancient ceremony after ancient ceremony, I could only feel sorry for archaeologists who can only describe a village they are uncovering as being so large, and constructed in such a way, or a stone monument as being of such a shape and size. A town is only a place this way. But to be able to know the name and use of particular areas, and then to conduct ceremonies that were once conducted here hundreds of years ago—now the town suddenly becomes alive and exists once more. And you become part of that town, and begin to learn some of its secrets.

Our first ceremony was conducted at a very strangely carved rock about five feet tall but cut and shaped with many unusual curves. This rock is called "The Hitching Post To The Sun" by most books but we considered it to be "The Doorway To The Center Of The Spirit." The first thing that don Edwardo asked us to do was to look at the shape of the large flat rock that "The Doorway" was sitting on. None of my guide books or books about this place even mentioned it. And yet, as you studied it, you suddenly realized that this base rock was an almost exact reproduction of the shape of the continent of South America! How could the Incas, who were supposed to be a fairly localized culture, have been able to know what the shape of the huge continent of South America was? And how long had they known this? Fascinating questions! Our ceremony lasted perhaps 20 or 30 minutes, and included kneeling in an unusually shaped niche in this rock while the group surrounding the stone chanted.

From this wonderful stone, considered the "male" stone, we went to the "female" stone called the "Pacha Mama" or Mother Earth stone. This is a much larger stone than "The Doorway," perhaps 12 or 15 feet wide and probably 10 feet tall. This time the shaman asked us to stand some distance in front of the stone and compare it's shape to that of the surrounding mountains. It's shape matched that of the distant mountain tops! What better way to represent Mother Earth than to follow her contours!

The ceremony here was longer and much more powerful (at least for me) than at "The Doorway." While standing in two columns in front of this stone chanting we each took our turn walking up to this huge stone. Standing in front of "her," facing the participants and then the rock, and with our arms outstretched, we presented the participants, and the rock, and the area, with wildflowers we had picked earlier. The feeling of power and oneness with Pacha Mama was very strong, and my chanting became similarly very strong, almost drowning out all the others.

From here we went to a large, perhaps 10 foot long, fairly flat stone that didn't seem to have a name. We were told by don Edwardo that participants are said to have lain on it with arms positioned slightly away from the body. From that position soul flight was believed to become possible—that is, travel without the body. Could this be how they learned the shape of the South American continent?

From here we went to the "Temple of the Seven Masters" followed by the "Condor" stone—a large rock in the ground but with its visible portion carved into that of a great condor. We also stopped at a small stone with a top carved at about a 45 degree angle which depicted the star constellation of the Southern Cross. In the afternoon we went to the Temple of the Falcon, where some of us and don Edwardo tried to contact the rest of our group, who had climbed to the top of the near-by mountain, by mental telepathy. We were constantly interrupted by other visitors coming in and talking during the meditation, so results were not very successful.

That evening we hiked up to the "Death Canoe," a large, very specially carved rock about 10 feet long and perhaps 5 feet wide, for the most powerful ceremony at this place of powerful ceremonies. Laying flat on our back on this stone, with arms fully outstretched, with the other members of the group standing around in a circle chanting, in total darkness, and in the pouring rain, we each in turn were ceremonially "killed" by the shaman plunging a dagger into our heart. Our spirit was then carried by the canoe to heaven followed by its return, still on the canoe, as a new and reborn person.

That is what is supposed to have happened. And it may have. But there were problems. First, Machu Picchu is at an elevation of about 7000 feet and the nights get cold there, even in summer. Add to that the fact that a cold rain began to fall precisely as we started the ceremony. Now such a thing is spiritually auspicious, since the rain can wash the spirit, as well as the body, clean. Unfortunately, because the rain didn't start until we started the ceremony, none of us wanted to break the circle to get our rain gear which lay only a few feet away. So there we were, standing in the circle chanting, in total darkness and cold rain, slowly getting soaked. Now your turn comes. You climb up on the stone and lay down on it. While before only your arms and shoulders were wet, now suddenly you are laying on a large stone running with water and your whole front is now getting rained on. Add to that, the fact that on this trip I was wearing a small quartz crystal in the form of a pyramid around my neck, and for some perverse reason, the pyramid was pointing down towards my heart. When the shaman, after due ceremony, plunged the ceremonial dagger into my heart, he hit that quartz pyramid dead on, and I was sure that he was using a real knife and had gone too far!

About midnight the ceremony ended and while some wanted to stay up there in a small nearby building, many of us now only wanted to dry out, take a warm shower, and climb into bed. In order to do this we had to find our way back down to the hotel outside of the ancient city, in total darkness (the small flashlights that some of us had were almost useless), in the mud, on very slippery rocks, and on a very steep slope. We finally made it without too many falls, only to find that the gate was locked. We had to wait in the rain for another twenty or thirty minutes while the shaman's apprentice climbed over the gate and tried to find the night watchman to let us out.

I had no reservations at the hotel but they fortunately had a few rooms left. So at last I got a heavenly warm shower and went to bed. Except suddenly now began one of the most profound happenings of a whole trip full of happenings! I had felt very little at "The Death Canoe" (except, of course, for the stab of pain from that pyramid when it tried to become part of me, literally as well as figuratively), but as I now relaxed in the warm bed I began to feel a very strange energy starting to surround my head. It grew stronger and stronger until I felt sure that my head must be glowing like a small sun! It then just continued to glow. Minute after minute it went on. I didn't try to see it by opening my eyes so I don't know if it was a physical glow or just a psychic one. However, I was so enthralled with it that I just "watched" it as the observer, looking for variations, curious at how long it would last, enjoying this very strange and wonderful feeling of light flowing through, and around, and from me.

It must have lasted for fifteen minutes or more, then it gradually diminished and disappeared, only to begin again in both of my hands! There it followed the same cycle, gradually increasing in intensity, staying for perhaps ten minutes or so and then gradually decreasing into nothingness. Even though I think I could have easily opened my eyes to look at my hands during this episode, for some reason I chose not to, rather depending on the sense of feel than on the sense of sight. There was no fear of any kind—just the wonderful knowledge of this extraordinary occurrence.

We traveled back to Cuzco and then to Lima the next day and then flew over the Andes to Pucalpa at the headwaters of the mighty Amazon. Here we were met by Augustin Rivas, an Amazonian shaman. At a jungle retreat, an hour's boat trip from the town, we held our last ceremony. "It is in the thick of the Amazon, the last remaining sanctuary on Earth, that one loses fear and finds one's power and inner peace. We will discover within each of us the spirit of the Shaman Warrior, the impeccable individual who has no enemies in this world or the next, and whose words and actions bring harmony and balance to the Earth." So says the Four Winds Foundation brochure. I'm not yet sure whether this all happened or not but certainly something happened to some of us.

This ceremony was scheduled to take place in the jungle village of A. Rivas, working with "his" stream and "his" trees. Unfortunately the Amazon was in full flood stage at this time, and to get there would have required us to wade in water up to our armpits with snakes and alligators as possible companions. For some reason we all declined to subject the snakes, etc., to our presence, so we held the ceremony near the lodge we were staying at instead.

The ceremony this time used an infusion of the ayahuasca or "death vine" to push along development. I, and several others, chose not to take any of this fluid, but took part in the rest of the ceremony. The purpose of this strange compound is to spiritually and psychically purify the interior of the body— and it does this with a vengeance. Within about 15 minutes of taking it, fluids start to flow out of every orifice of the body and fortunately there are men and women helpers present to help the individuals get rid of this problem as easily and with as much discreteness as possible. After the physical problems subside there is apparently a halucinigenic effect. After the ceremony I was helping one of the women who had taken it, back to her room, and she kept asking me if I saw the beautiful lights and glow between the boards on the walkways. In addition to our group there were several people from the surrounding area who were there to be healed. One of our members also had cancer and, after trying more usual treatments, took this trip primarily to see if it would help her. I have no knowledge about how any of these cases turned out.

I personally felt nothing from this particular ceremony, even though it lasted for more than two hours. Incidentally, in addition to being one of the most famous shaman in the area, A. Rivas is also a professional sculptor, working in jungle materials. I have one of his jungle animal heads in my den and enjoy it every time I see it.

While flying from Lima to Miami, via the Amazon region, I had another very strange experience. I was sitting at one of the airplane windows and was just relaxing and watching the jungle go by when suddenly I felt myself literally become an eagle, flying over the jungle below! It was so real that I could literally feel the wind as it whistled over my outstretched wings. I remember soaring back and forth over the jungle below, catching the wind, flapping my wings to go higher or just swooping down to go lower. It was absolutely magnificent—so free, and comfortable, and easy, as I wheeled over the jungle canopy.

Finally I flew lower, selected a large branch to alight on and then I could actually feel my talons bite into the tree branch as I landed on it. I have no idea how long this lasted and I am relatively sure I wasn't asleep. If I was, I have never had such a realistic dream—not only seeing what was happening but actually feeling it as well. It was so real that even today, more than three years after it happened, I can still feel the wind flowing over my outstretched wings as I soar over the jungle. And, as I write this, I can still feel my talons grab onto that branch. I have never had a dream even come close to being remembered that long. I usually forget them within minutes of waking up, and I can't ever remember one lasting longer than a day!

PART II
DIALOGUES WITH AN ASCENDED MASTER
(1988-1993)

CHAPTER 9

FIRST CONTACT WITH DK

Between my last meditation contact on April 1, 1979 and the next statement in my journal on June 1988, more than 9 years later, no entries were made in it. However, as previously indicated, I had been traveling with a vengeance. I had also continued meditation up until about 1985. At that time, I found that I was in a more or less continuous meditation. The formal act of meditating no longer seemed to be required, though it was still used when a need for it was felt. Study continued during this time, integrated into my travels.

The reason for digging out the diary, after the second trip to Peru in April, 1988, was a strange transmission in June, 1988 which really got my attention. That entry says simply: "Awoke with 'You are now free from the tyranny of sex.'" An interesting transmission to say the least, and isn't "tyranny" an interesting word to be used in conjunction with the word "sex"?

On September 5, 1988 we were again using the Ouija Board to try to determine why I hadn't found the address in New York City, when a name and telephone number (with area code) suddenly came through, and with a message telling me to call it on a specific date (see chapter 7).

On September 16, 1988, as directed, I called the person and number specified. Remember, I didn't know who he/she was or why I was to call. You can imagine what that call sounded like: "I don't know who you are or why I am calling you but an Ouija Board gave me your name and telephone number and told me to call you on this date!"

It turned out that the person that I was told to call, M. Luria, was a spiritual channel for **DK**. She had been on a vacation for several weeks and just returned the day before. Therefore, if I had not waited for that day to call her, no one would have been there and I probably would have given up after trying several times. As we talked I found out that she had become a spiritual channel for **DK** about a year previously. I, on the other hand, had been studying the 20 or so books of **DK** as channeled through Alice A. Bailey (during the period of about 1922 to about 1960 and published by the Lucis Publishing Co. of NYC) for the last twenty years. These were easily the best books I have ever found in this field. Their only problem was that they were so precise, and so thorough, that I seldom understood them nearly as much as I thought I should. I had also spent about 12 years working with the Arcane School, which is based largely on the teachings of **DK**. What a revelation for me to find such a capability in someone—and so near as well? I wasn't even aware that anyone had been channeling him since Alice Bailey's death in the 1960's.

Well, I have quoted **DK** many times in this book so far, as giving me very special and usually very exciting answers and guidance. But just who is he?

DK, also known as The Tibetan or Djwhal Khul, or the Ascended Master Djwhal Khul or sometimes as the philosopher of the Masters, describes himself as the following: (Given to me in October, 1991 as this book is being written)

"I am a being who has served God for thousands of years. I am one of the 'helpers' of the Spiritual Hierarchy

and am currently helping direct the ascension of mankind through another of their many 'leaps' into a newer and greater being. I do this by 'pushing' and 'shoving' and otherwise 'dragging' individuals into knowledge which they will hopefully use for the betterment and growth of mankind. It is a difficult and frustrating 'job' because humans are 'such individuals' that they want to believe that everything that they 'think' is theirs and useable for just their own growth and enrichment and enjoyment and profit rather than for the good of, and growth of, all humanity. Accordingly ideas must be given out extremely carefully, especially major new ideas which can effect major numbers of humanity.

"Mankind in the past has grown from extremely primitive beings to their present state because there have been enough individuals who were more concerned with mankind than their individual benefit to make such leaps possible. (Such 'leaps' are the result of mental as well as physical changes). Now there are so many individuals on Earth that unless we not only give out ideas, but also help nurture the ideas, they are likely to be lost in the shuffle, and even then many are lost or so changed that they are hopeless for what we hoped for.

"The words printed in this book are another attempt to help mankind make this next critical step by giving out information which can make this next Transition somewhat easier than previous Transitions. We have given more information here than usual and made it easier to understand in the hope that its value will be realized and made use of for, and by, all."

The words "Spiritual Hierarchy" were mentioned in these comments. **DK** defines this group as follows:

"This is a spiritual organization, sometimes also called 'The Brotherhood,' which interacts with God to try to carry out plans for the growth of mankind as laid down at the formation of the Earth. Members are typically not physically present on Earth although they may occasionally take a physical form by incarnating on Earth for a particular lifetime and time period. As discussed further in this book, they typically work through individuals on Earth by placing situations or ideas before, or in, carefully selected individuals and then step back to see what happens. In this manner they attempt to guide the growth of mankind and help it to, when ready, grow and progress up the ladder of spiritual development. But always without taking away mankind's inalienable right of self-determination."

(HK note: This definition is essentially the same as that given on page 40. It was included here to show the uniformity of transmissions.)

Getting back now to my discussion with M. Luria. After her first shock at being mentioned by an Ouija Board, she made an appointment for me to come to her home (which was just a few miles from where I worked!) so I could meet and talk directly to **DK** through her.

Shortly after our conversation, M. Luria gave a course on how to channel—which I took. During this course I began channeling **DK** myself. Apparently I channel on a somewhat different level of contact than M. Luria, however. While she is also a conscious channel, not gong into a "trance" when channeling, I not only maintain full consciousness while channeling, but now require no setting aside of the ego or even closing of the eyes (although I sometimes do this to reduce the flood of information reaching the brain.) For instance, I am even able to drive a car while a conversation between us goes on.

For this meeting I had drawn up several questions that I

wanted to ask him so you will note that every once in awhile in the discussion a new topic is introduced, even though we may not have quite finished his previous answers. This was done because I was trying to get through all of my questions in the 45 minutes we were to have together. What follows is a repeat of our conversation on that day made from a tape we made, as transcribed by a professional stenographer:

Sept. 16, 1988, 10-10:45 AM: **DK** to HK through M. Luria:

DK: "Good afternoon. And how are you today?"

HK: "Fine, thank you."

DK: "Oh, indeed you are. Do you realize how fine you are?"

HK: "No, I do not."

DK: "Well, you know, there are times when you've gotten a glimpse of your own radiance factor, haven't you?"

HK: "Occasionally."

DK: "And what do you do with these glimpses?"

HK: "I don't really know. I think about them, but then I forget them."

DK: "You might remember them, because every time you get one of those glimpses a veil drops or is lifted, however you wish to look at it. And you might say you're getting very close to literally breaking through some veils of perception in terms of the third eye focus and in terms of really being able to, you might say, experience a measurable increase in your awareness of your light factor. So what you might do on a daily basis is to really say, 'How do I access my radiance today? How do I access the brilliance or the effect of the light flow as it moves through me?' Bring your attention to it on a daily basis. Play with it.

Have some fun with it. Because now you are getting ready to really lighten immeasurably. All right, what would you like to know?"

HK: "I would like to know how I may best help the Hierarchy during the rest of my life?"

DK: "Well, what would you like to do?"

HK: "I'm not really sure. I've enjoyed writing more than I thought I would, and I would like to try to raise the consciousness of people if possible."

DK: "What do you understand about channeling?"

HK: "Very little. I wasn't aware of it until about a year ago. I'm just starting to learn that there is such a thing and I've become fascinated by it."

DK: "All right. You might say that you're going to have an opportunity to really work with a scientific basis for the channel. Do you know what I am saying? How do you suppose that might occur?"

HK: "I would suppose by my allowing a person-an entity-to take over my body-or be partially taken over."

DK: "Yes, and at the same time to use-you might say-your particular filter or your particular frame of reference to really, well, the word could be 'legitimize' it, but that's not really the word I wish to use. You might say to bring the non-linear function into the realm that the rational mind can come to terms with. Do you understand this? And that is useful in your own process as well, isn't it? Because that is what you are doing, isn't it? You are marrying the two functions, aren't you? And that is kind of exciting you see. All right, now as far as the next step, well, that is it isn't it? Now, how do you wish to go about that?"

HK: "I don't know. That is why I'm talking to you."

DK: "I know, but I like to stimulate your imagination a little bit. All right. What do you think might be involved in

really putting a rational framework-an understanding-in communicating what a channel is all about?"

HK: "I don't know. I don't have an answer to that."

DK: "All right. This is an old habit of mine you know. Back in the old days together in Tibet-you know we spent some time together there-I used to ask you questions and it really wasn't for you to come forth with an answer. It was for you to just enjoy the question. What do you suppose questions do?"

HK: "They make you think."

DK: "Yes. Sometimes they make your mind break down, don't they?' And that's helpful, isn't it? What happens when the mind breaks down?"

HK: "Then new channels are opened."

DK: "You've got it. You see, then you get to bridge from the new place to the old, don't you? That is what you are about to do-to build a bridge. And that is how you can help the Hierarchy. Because, you see, what's occurring on the old plane right now is a lack of opening potentiality among the collective consciousness and that means that-well-it would be very useful and helpful to the planet for-you might say-the collective mass-to come to a different alignment with their higher selves. To come into a different alignment with source flow. And that means opening the channel. Now that's happening quite a bit on the fringe, isn't it? But it is a matter of a lot of people looking at that and saying, 'Well, that's not valid' or 'Well, that's for the poets. That it isn't for the mainstream.' Well, it's time for the mainstream to really shift beyond their egos. Do you understand?

"In order to be able to walk the streets and be among many enlightened beings-which is right around the corner-there must be a collective shift in terms of having it be a very ordinary-not extraordinary-but ordinary experience to come from the channel focus which involves, of course, the going beyond the ego and living beyond the ego. Are you willing to interact with this process?"

HK: "Absolutely!"

DK: "Good. All right. That is your assignment. So why don't we start there? How would you describe your relationship with your ego at this point in the process?"

HK: "I don't know how to describe it."

DK: "Oh, give it a try."

HK: "We discuss-and argue-I suspect. I don't know what else one can say. We don't get along sometimes."

DK: "All right. Who is in charge?"

HK: "Oh, usually the ego, I suspect."

DK: "Yes. And what is your awareness of what is possible in terms of that?"

HK: "Oh, there are unlimited possibilities."

DK: "All right. How would you scientifically describe-in a linear fashion-the process of going beyond the ego?"

HK: "I don't know how to describe that."

DK: "All right. Well, that is good. You've got the tape (of this conversation). You can work on that. Because through your channel you can bring or create a description. You can work with that in such a way that you'll be able to communicate the incommunicable—communicate the mystery and put it in a form that can be communicated. That is very necessary at this point on the Earth plane.

"You might say that the time is now to really go beyond the ego—and to move into an understanding of what it is like to live through the point of a channel—meaning in alignment with the higher self. It is the same thing. And to give substantiality so that others can follow. And you agree to pioneer some of that? You agree to pioneer it in a way

that can be heard by others that are perhaps mostly oper-
ating from a rational or linear mode?

"Would you like to write a book about the process of
opening the channel? Would you like to write a book about
substantiating formlessness?

"You-and others-have crossed a bridge. You're standing on the other side and you're waving to the collective
consciences and you're saying, 'Come on over. It's fine
here. As a matter of fact, there are some treasures here.'
But from where the collective consciences stand, they don't
see it. There is a veil there. It is part of your agreement, if
you are willing to participate, to help lift that veil and
substantiate what is on the other side. And substantiate it in
a way that is hearable to the mainstream. Do you understand?

"I would suggest that it would be useful perhaps to
really document you own experiences of channeling. What
do you see in your own process of opening to channel?"

HK: "I don't see anything."

DK: "Oh yes you do. Take a look."

HK: "I don't feel I've ever done it before. It is very difficult."

**DK: "Yes, well, you can take the struggle out of it. I
know you like the challenge. But take some of the struggle
out of it. Play with it. It's a game. All right, you've already
channeled, haven't you?"**

HK: "I must have?"

**DK: "Of course. You see? Now if it is that natural what
does it tell you?"**

HK: "It tells me I can do it."

DK: "And what else does it tell you?"

HK: "It tells me it isn't the problem I thought it would be."

DK: "Good. As a matter of fact, it's not even that big a

deal. And what is it that makes it a big deal?"

HK: "The unknown. It seems so strange."

DK: "Good. Now, how does the ego react to the unknown?"

HK: "It's afraid of it."

DK: "Yes. So fear enters into it, doesn't it?"

HK: "Very much so."

DK: "And what does fear do to the channel?"

HK: "Fear stops it."

DK: "Yes, fear closes the channel. Can you describe this in terms of energy?"

HK: "Certainly there is an expansion or increase in it during channeling. More energy flowing-and then shutting off when fear enters."

DK: "All right. The idea is to do this kind of thing. In other words, experiment with your channel. Experiment with the effect that the emotional body has on it at its energetic level. Experiment with expansion and contraction. Experiment with what happens when you take the channel and, you might say, you send it out, kind of like sending out from a TV antennae. And what is it? Draw it in and give a name to it. Provide evidence for it. Make it real in a way that others can hear the realness of it, although none of it is real, you see.

"It's a dream on the Earth plane, but it's a convincing dream. What we are trying to do is wake everybody up. We are trying to enlighten the planet. That is what the Brotherhood is trying to do right now. And the planet is working on enlightening herself. Now that means waking others up from a dream, and that involves first substantiating their dream and then in assisting them in going beyond the dream. Understand? Questions?"

HK: "Could I perhaps channel Beethoven and continue

writing a symphony for him?"

DK: "Why not-if you like."

HK: "Would it be worthwhile?"

DK: "Well, when you say, 'Worthwhile,' what do you mean exactly?"

HK: "To help people grow . To help them understand what is possible."

DK: "You know, it is kind of interesting. It's a fine balance between others looking at something extraordinary and getting attached to it. What happens to that extraordinariness is that they feel they need that in order to go beyond their ordinariness. In actuality what you might do is to draw the entire experience down into an ordinary focus so they can claim that for their own experience.

"Because it is not the extraordinary that is going to awaken the planet-not at this point, you see. Back a few thousand years ago it was necessary. Now it is a matter of the ordinariness in terms of the entire collective consciousness shifting. There has to be a way to assist others in knowing that they can claim these experiences and this reality for themselves. It is not a guru out there, or an enlightened master over there. You don't see many gurus these days."

HK: "No you don't. And those you see aren't very good either."

DK: "Good. Well yes, there is a reason for that. What do you suppose that reason is?"

HK: "They aren't necessary."

DK: "Good. It's individualization time, isn't it? It is time to really assist, through your own experience of drawing back in. So if you channel a way to preserve or complete one of Beethoven's pieces-well, that may be convincing on one level, but on another level perhaps it may be

more useful for you to substantiate this process through a personal focus. Substantiate this process perhaps more immediately in terms of how does one hook into one's higher self? Because that is really the key. Not everyone will be able to tap into Beethoven's energy, depending on their channel and their senses-and it doesn't really matter, does it? What matters is that they open; what matters is that they align; what matters is that they go beyond ego, and that they are willing to clear the myriad of false beliefs connected to all kinds of fears about the unknown. Because what is happening on the Earth plane right now is that there is a great shift in terms of the feminine flow of source coming forth.

"What do you suppose is involved in that feminine flow? The feminine flow has to do with, you might say, the dark side of source or the void. And the void holds the mystery, doesn't it? In order to tap into the channel focus, one must go into the void, go into that receptivity. Now the ego doesn't like that and gets kind of alarmed. That is the bridge you are building. You can substantiate that in a way that others can hear, from your own experience, through your own expertise. Then you put it together and in an ordinary focus so that others can resonate with it."

HK: "I would like to write a book summarizing your books so that they might reach a broader group and have an easier understanding. Is that a good idea?"

DK: "Why don't you just draw me through and why don't you channel a fresh book? Those previous books stretched some of the collective mental focus and that was useful. But life now is a little different, isn't it? There is not so much time for that kind of intellectualism. You see, this is the time for immediacy of experience. And that is what wants to come forth right now. It is a time to wake up

NOW! And therefore, it is really a time for focusing alignment in all of the bodies, you see? Rather than perhaps, stimulating to such an extent the mental body. And that is what you are aware of. You have that awareness. So what you might do is work with your channel, and we can work together, you and I, and draw something fresh in that will be really more involved with actual, hands-on assisting that experience of going beyond ego and moving into the alignment, you see?"

HK: "How do we open up that channel between you and me?"

DK: "What do you suppose is the biggest block that would affect your channel?"

HK: "Well, I know its possible. I suspect there is part of my ego that says it really isn't possible."

DK:"Yes, you've got it. What is the ego saying when it says that?"

HK: "I think it is probably fear more than anything else."

DK: "Yes. It is fear of its own destruction. How do you suppose you can work with your ego?"

HK: "I'm sure I can't use brute force. It must be a very delicate approach."

DK: "Good. You've got that one right. Because the ego is part of your divinity, isn't it? It is not something to be negated by any stretch of the imagination. It is a matter of really lovingly and compassionately working with the ego and treating it as if it were a child. And really, very carefully, well, you might say appreciating its process, because it must step down, but not be extinguished. It is useful to put on an ego, you see. It is necessary on the Earth plane to put one on. It's the way you identify each other. But the point is that it not be in charge.

"Now the first thing you can notice is that whenever

you have needs you're dealing with the ego, aren't you? You can begin to really examine closely what your ego looks like. You can say, 'What is the face of my ego? How does it put forth its needs? How does it express its needs? How does it need to be important? How does it need to be diminished? How does it need to be in control?' Now control is the issue here, isn't it? All of these questions, and their answers, are really a way for you to acquaint yourself, to really know the ego, because you cannot master it unless you know it. And this is a process of mastering the ego, isn't it?

"Really ask for the ego to input to you. And it will because egos love attention. Simply say, 'Input to me now about how you feel about the fact that I'm going to jump into the void here.' Pay attention-and you really might want to take some notes on what occurs at the ego level-so you can really begin to map out the entire process of the ego's response to this very necessary shift in the awareness process and how to work with that. Always come forth with a loving, compassionate response to the ego."

HK: "Should I continue to try to open the third eye?"

DK: "Why not? How do you do that?"

HK: "I don't know how. That's one of the reasons I'm here."

DK: "How do you work with that?"

HK: "I simply try to put my consciousness up into the third eye."

DK: "All right. And what occurs?"

HK: "Nothing!"

DK: "Well, so you think. It's kind of interesting. Why don't you decide that first and foremost that it is the ego speaking when you decide that nothing happens? Now once you get that out of the way you're free to see what is happening. Now it is subtle. When you are in this world you are working with subtle energies aren't you? And, therefore, it's kind of like trying to look out of the corner of your eye at it. You can't take it on directly, can you? And that gets kind of interesting. So the first thing you might do is say to yourself, 'Every time I bring my attention and my realm to the third eye, something happens-because it does. Secondly, it is not something that is knowable to me as I know reality. Good, I can let go of that. Thirdly, I can allow myself to experience the subtle realm.'

"What you might do in your meditation is align yourself and take some deep breaths, and you might take in some light from the back of the third eye. And you project it, as if it were a movie camera, right out of the screen onto the inside of the forehead where the third eye is-between the two eyebrows. Don't push it. Part of it is going to be a softening process.

"You're fairly comfortable with that Yang or masculine energy, aren't you? But how do you feel about the Yin or feminine energy? It's tricky for you, isn't it? Well, that's all right, but it is an important process for you right now. That is, becoming more comfortable with that Yin or that receptive mode, that feminine flow. And so, some times you push it kind of hard, and then it's hard to grasp because the creative process takes both flows, doesn't it?

"You see, in order for creation to take place you have to have the emptiness, or the womb, or the void. That's the feminine energy, you see. And that is potentiality unmanifested. From that springs forth the doing, or the action, the male focus. And so what you want to do, before you undertake any process, is to move first into the emptiness. That is your foundation for creation, you see. You are going to be doing a lot of channeling through your third eye. So what you want to do is to first say, 'I'm going to empty completely and I'm going to literally soften every aspect of my physical being. I'm going to soften the heart chakra, and I'm going to move into a state of emptiness. And when I fill up with thoughts I'm going to pour them out. And when I begin to fill up with fears or emotions, I'm going to pour them out. I'm going to move as best as possible into a flow of void-of complete and total emptiness and cool darkness. I'm then going to allow myself to rest in that vast, vast potentiality of self.

"Really get comfortable in it. Now, your ego wants to do things. It wants to take charge, it wants to shape things. While there is a place for that Yang or male energy, it will be useful for you to build up a comfort level with the Yin aspect of self. Now you've already built it up to some extent, but you have to really stretch out into it now. What you want to do is really get comfortable with not knowing. And really get comfortable with emptiness. When you feel like you are literally floating in that wondrous void—then, and only then, draw in the light which is just the male side of source. Draw that light from the back of the head into the front. And let it touch, not penetrate, but touch the third eye. You don't want to penetrate it. You want to soften and dissolve and open it."

HK: "Should I do any more traveling?"

DK: "What would be the intention of such travel?"

HK: "To try to feel the energies at these places and to try to find hidden chambers."

DK: "If you were to see that as a mirror for your process, what would you see?"

HK: "Probably the treasure hunter in me."

DK: "You've got it. What treasures are you seeking within self?"

HK: "To grow. To expand. To become one with you."

DK: "Good. So they are treasures of awareness aren't they? They give you a freedom and travel that no external experience can give you, don't they? Well, if you want to actualize your process through physical movement, why not? But bear in mind that it is nothing more than a mirror. And that the hidden chambers are within you. As a matter of fact, there's one in each of your chakras. Especially the heart chakra. How is that going?"

HK: "Slowly."

DK: "You might want to work more with that. How do you work with your heart chakra?"

HK: "I simply think about it and try to spin it. I don't know much more about what I should do."

DK: "What happens when you do that?"

HK: "Nothing. I feel nothing."

DK: "Throw that away. What you might really do is say, 'All right. I'm going to really open this part. What I'm going to do is in my imagination. (And use your imagination. Have fun with it) Once again, deep breathe, relax the body, and bring awareness into the heart chakra. (You've got some interesting blockages in the back of the chakra.) And what you might do—well two things. First of all from the back of the chakra you might envision yourself two inches high with a flashlight that sheds source flow through its light. And you might begin to, through your imagination (It's a very powerful tool. You're not convinced of that yet, but that's all right.) you might flood that energy in the back of the heart. You might begin to really flood that light and literally begin to dissolve some of that scar tissue there (You've got some scar tissue there-energetically speaking. You've been in a fair amount of wars in your past lives. You've been shot in the back a few times.) It is an interest-

129

ing thing with the heart because the heart is essentially—
You have a great deal of trust, don't you?"

HK: "Yes"

DK: "At the same time sometimes you feel as if you must wear a shield."

HK: "Yes"

DK: "There is nothing wrong with that except that sometimes it's nice not to have to wear a shield. So what you might do is work with dissolving some of that 'stuff' in the back of the chakra. (By the way, did you know that you intake through the back of the chakra?) When you get all the way through you might sit in the heart chakra. Just sit in it and its field of light. And what you might do is allow yourself to bask in those energies of Love. Let them soften you as if you were taking a shower or bath. And listen to the heart's wisdom.

"And what you might do is to bring a particular question to the heart and tap on its wisdom. In the future-well, actually you can do this now as you're working on your channel-you can call me and I'll meet you in the heart. We'll do a lot of work in the third eye, but it is useful to meet in the heart because there is a trust, and there is also love."

HK: "Next question. Are there any things about myself that I should know that would help me grow better in this current life? And how about the same question concerning past lives?"

DK: "Well, you've always been somewhat more comfortable in male bodies than female bodies. Do you know why?"

HK: "No."

DK: "Because you've always wanted to demonstrate light-source light. You've always wanted to demonstrate it. Put it forth through action, through some form of doing.

And why not? And that has been useful to you. Because you've developed a-you might say-a well developed creative function in terms of being able to actualize or manifest on the Earth plane these kinds of experience. Well, it would be very useful for you now to really move into your 'beingness' versus your 'doingness.' What does that mean to you?"

HK: "I think it means becoming less active. To sit back and relax and feel and stop thinking that something has to be done immediately."

DK: "Good. What do you suppose you would learn from that?"

HK: "Certainly temperance and relaxation and perhaps growth and understanding of the other portions of myself."

DK: "And perhaps you would learn-you might say you would experience-a level of 'knowingness' of self out of the realm of doing-which would put you into your 'beingness.' What it would do would be to assist you in getting beyond some old programming that you have that you must achieve in order to be enlightened. Do you know that programming?"

HK: "No"

DK: "Well, you might consider it. It's a possibility. How do you suppose enlightenment really occurs?"

HK: "It has always occurred in me through very hard work and long waiting."

DK: "All right. Well, you're remembering some past lives. One time we were working together and I tried to get you to sit still, then too. I had you go out into nature and really try to understand the true essence of things as nature presents them. And you did your best to really sit with it. But what happened is that because you couldn't perceive at that point the subtle level of your own process, what occurred was that you turned it against yourself and you thought, 'This is going to be hard work and this is going to be a struggle.' Now that struggle theme kind of 'cooked' into you a little bit-subconsciously, you see, and you decided that ascending or moving into that elevated place of enlightenment was, as you said, the result of a lot of hard work and long waiting. But there was a certain amount of despair there, that you could actually ever do that. You were wondering if you had what it took."

HK: "Yes, I still have that."

DK: "I know. That is why we are discussing it right now. It's time to let that go. Why don't I give you a simple technique for removing some false beliefs.? Basically I'll suggest a few false beliefs you've got stored at the subconscious level as a result of some past life flows. Write these down on a piece of paper. As you say each one out loud, envision a light-filled hand going into the crown chakra and removing a stone that correlates to that particular false belief. To remove it throw the stone (held by the light-filled hand) against a concrete wall and watch it explode. This is a simple Tibetan technique for clearing. Now for you and using this technique say:

"Please remove: Enlightenment is a difficult and arduous process.

"Please remove: I do not yet have what it takes to open that door to enlightenment.

"Please remove: I must endure long and painful waiting in order to be enlightened.

"Please remove: I cannot sit still long enough to perceive my true nature.

"Please remove: If I allow myself to move into that Yin or that feminine flow side of self, I won't do what is required in order to be enlightened.

"Please remove: To be enlightened requires doing.

"Please remove: I will not experience my enlightenment in this life time.

"Please remove: Enlightenment is a distant vision that has not yet developed itself.

"Now do you know what we are talking about here? We are talking about you really considering your enlightenment process. NOW! Not then, but NOW! And the way you're going to do it is in your own unique way. That is not the way Buddha did it—and you were fascinated by Buddha. But he did it his way, didn't he? And you are going to do it your way. And it is for you to discover and to create your path and to really discern and to accept your own energies. Now it will require some balancing into that feminine flow. Some allowingness. Some receptivity. Some letting go of the doing and the struggle and the hard work. It is easy on one level and it is an organic unfoldment that is available to you. When you really get that in your heart, you trust that. Then what will occur will be a balance of the male and female energies within you. And then all kinds of fun things begin to happen."

HK: "How often should I talk to you through this channel?"

DK: "As often as you like. You see, it's interesting, these kind of sittings—like is occurring right now. What you might do is go home with the tape and play it for awhile and work with some of the exercises. And you watch your process start to accelerate a little bit—not that it hasn't already. And when you really get to think of them more actively, you can come back and we can talk again."

HK: "Can I talk to you directly?"

DK: "That is what I am hoping for, so we can get to work on that book. Therefore, what I would really encourage you to do is to once again sit and still the body, then still the emotions and the mind as best as possible, and take that precious ego of yours and love it and gently put it aside somewhere. Then allow yourself to really feel, to really move into that emptiness and envision yourself as a pillar of light. And know that you are nothing more than a vessel. As you experience light pouring down through the crown chakra and down through your whole body, bring your awareness into the heart and call me forth. Don't worry whether it is real or not. That is secondary. It is all real and it's all not real. It doesn't matter.

"When you call me forth in the heart you might see me coming toward you in my light body and perhaps we'll experience some kind of reunion. And then, probably, we'll do some work. What we'll do is we'll bring awareness, we'll bring mixed energies to the third eye focus. And you can draw that light into the back of the head. What you might do before you call me forth is have some questions. You might also have a tape recorder handy because when you're in the channel focus it's kind of hard to retain all the information. So you might pose a question. Now comes the fun part-allowing me to answer. It means waiting. It means listening. And that is when the ego is going to get all kinds of excited. And it (the ego) is going to say things like, 'This isn't working.' and 'You can't do it. It's not real. It's not justifiable. It's not measurable.' It's going to input to you and you must gently put it aside and really allow yourself to speak forth anything that comes to you. You know, growing the channel is just like anything else. It's like getting into shape. You just do it and do it and do it. And it gets better and better. So if you commit to doing it a lot you'll stretch right into it. And we can talk quite a lot because we've made a connection. Well, we have been working together on the other planes for quite a long time. But your ego gets to participate in this connection."

HK: "Fine but I'm a slow learner."

DK: "Well, what do you mean by that?"

HK: "It seems to take me forever to learn what other people learn so rapidly."

DK: "If you consider that time is an illusion, it hardly matters, does it? Also, why do you suppose you came to the conclusion that you're a slow learner?"

HK: "I think simply watching things happen and comparing myself to others."

DK: "It's that comparison, isn't it?"

HK: "That is it, yes. It's a killer."

DK: "Please remove: I must compare myself to others in order to access my process and progress. That is kind of what snafooed you back in Tibet when we were together. Because you were looking out there and you looked at Buddha and you looked at other enlightened beings. You looked at me for that matter. Guess what you thought of yourself?"

HK: "That I was nothing."

DK: "You got it. And you know, when you think you are nothing it's hard to access your magnitude, isn't it? And that is why it is very useful for you now to clear out those false beliefs about being nothing. And to really allow yourself to move into your magnitude, to move into your potentiality. And to know that your becoming process is truly happening. And that it is not at all useful for you to measure it according to others."

HK: "May I ask you how my diet is doing? Should I retain it, or does it need changes?"

DK: "Why don't you describe your diet for the channel."

HK: "I'm using your diet, the one you wrote about in your book "Initiation, Human and Solar" (A. A. Bailey, Lucis Publishing Co., Chapt. 19, Rule 6, pg 196) where you said "—each disciple be strictly vegetarian" and about a year ago I also stopped eating eggs and cheese as well."

DK: "And how do you feel?"

HK: "I feel wonderful. Full of energy."

DK: "Then what would you want to change?"

HK: "I don't want to change anything unless changing something might help me."

DK: "Not really. You might say at this point that there is really nothing at the physical level that could really get in the way, so to speak. You might say the biggest thing would be for you to stop."

HK: "Stop what?"

DK: "Everything. Do you know what I mean?"

HK: "No, I really don't know what you mean."

DK: "Well, what do you suppose I mean?"

HK: "Stop thinking about it, I suspect. Stop worrying and being concerned about it."

DK: "Yes. What is the concern connected to?"

HK: "The concern, I suspect, is that the reason I use the diet is to help me grow, and that I won't be able to grow without using the diet."

DK: "Exactly. You've got it. Please remove: It is not essentially in my nature to become enlightened or to become realized, so I must do things or add things that will make it possible for self-enlightenment. When you throw that one away what happens—well, on one level it's kind of fun because it doesn't matter what you do. But on another level some things do assist you while you're working on your mastery. In other words, until you master the physical, it's useful to eat properly. Once you master it, it doesn't

matter what you eat, you see? All right. Until you master the emotional body it is useful to work with the emotions, accepting them and allowing them to work with you. Once you master the emotional body, it doesn't matter. You can put on anger at the drop of a hat. It doesn't really matter because you're not attached to it, you see? All right. Now for you, it's interest with the mental body, isn't it? Because in many ways you want to know. Can you let go of your attachment to know?"

HK: "That would be more difficult but I hope I can do that."

DK: "How can you do that?"

HK: "Simply stop worrying and being concerned with it. Stop trying to write everything down that might tell me something that I might forget."

DK: "So it really is a matter of allowing yourself to not know. Now what do you suppose would happen if you allowed yourself to not know?"

HK: "Actually it happens many times every day that I realize that I don't know things."

DK: "And how do you respond to that?"

HK: "I try to learn them."

DK: "What if you allowed yourself to just not know? Do you know what it is? It boils down to this. You spend a lot of time acquiring knowledge, don't you? Then you get to spend some lifetimes letting go of it. Then when you truly know nothing you are free.

"Perhaps that is a good time to stop our conversation. It is a delight to sit with you and I look forward to working with you within your channel and we can do some good work together."

CHAPTER 10

THE CONTACTS CONTINUE

The following two chapters are very difficult for me to write. They include statements that are normally kept completely secret by the pupil. Furthermore, many are of such a nature that the most likely response of the reader will be one of disbelief. Many are unbelievable to me as well. However, on September 2, 1991 at 4:30 AM, I received the following message:

"The time has come to reveal yourself through words and deeds."

Therefore, as directed, I am writing, in the two following chapters, the contents of my journal for the last five years. If you are not specifically interested in the development of a disciple I would suggest that you skip Chapters 10 and 11 and go directly to Chapters 12, 13, and 14. These last three Chapters discuss the culmination of 25 years of work and teach our past and future history as well as a great deal of totally new information about the Earth and humanity and about God.

If you choose to read Chapters 10 and 11, please try to keep as open a mind as possible. They may be the most startling text you have ever read. After reading these Chapters, you will wonder "Can this possibly be true?" All I can say is that this is an exact transcription of what occurred. Since the story is not yet complete, I have no way of proving, or disproving, any of it. Perhaps, someday, something will occur which will allow us to finally know what the "truth" is concerning this information.

Following my First Contact with **DK** a whole new level of contact, information transfer and spiritual development began. This started about a week after the First Contact when on Sept.24, 1988 I noted in the journal: "Repeated energy inputs last night during sleep. Six to twelve times." (This is one of the places where you will be able to feel this energy by following the instructions in the Introduction)

On October 11, 1988, during my second class on "How to Channel" from M. Luria, I could vaguely see the aura around the head of one of the women students. It was extending out a distance of about 1/2 inch. (Not very far when you consider that the aura is reported to extend out well over a foot but this is the most intense region and probably a good place for beginners to start.) I have never seen an aura since this incident.

I also emptied my mind of the ego for the first time. What a surprise! I felt like a hollow cylinder after it was gone! (But the ego was back shortly—perhaps 15 minutes or so—and the empty feeling disappeared.) The next morning after emptying in the void as suggested by **DK**, I tingled all over, similar to what had happened in New York City.

On October 21, 1988 I had another very strong energy input, lasting all day, but especially powerful in the morning. The same happened again on October 25, 1988.

On Nov. 1, 1988, during our fifth class session I channeled knowingly for the first time.

During the evening of Nov. 2, 1988, using **DK**'s technique for meeting him in my heart chakra, we met for the first time. He had said during our discussion "When you call me forth in the heart you might see me coming toward you in my light body and perhaps we'll experience some kind of reunion." Was that an understatement! No matter what I write here I won't be able to fully describe what happened at that meeting! I wrote in my journal "What LOVE occurred! An all encompassing, overflowing of energy and light and LOVE. Indescribable!" But it was so much more than these words so inadequately convey! Can you imagine being enclosed in a bubble of Love? (Not physical love but spiritual Love) Every nerve in your body is tingling with wonder and yet so much more than even that. This lasted for many minutes. If you carefully follow my instructions in the Introduction you should be able to tap into this energy and actually feel at least part of what occurred at this meeting.

On Nov. 6, 1988 I channeled at home (in the morning) for the first time. I didn't record it, but it was concerned with the need for preparation for channeling to obtain the full benefits.

("Such preparation would typically include meditation and study for at least a year prior to opening the channel." (Nov.1991 input)).

On awakening the morning of November 11, 1988 (Note the date—111188) I had my first real thought transmission in many years, and more than 20 years after I began this study. It said:

"Today is the day of enlightenment. You are the first of a new group of enlightened beings. All the cells in your body were changed last night. There is no longer any need to eat although you can do so if you wish."

(HK note: Concerning this last statement, I now find myself eating less and less, although I still usually eat three small meals a day. My weight hasn't seemed to change at all even though I now eat probably less than half of what I used to eat.)

"You can now heal by touching your finger to the forehead of the person to be healed. You are to touch the forehead of each member of your channeling class to begin their enlightenment. As you touch each say, 'With this

touch I bring to you the clear white light of God and the pure golden light of LOVE to start your enlightenment process."

What can one say about such a statement? Is it true? How can one prove such a thing, even to oneself? I don't have an answer to such questions. I did, however, carry out the instructions and touch the forehead of each member of the class, and the instructor as well, giving the specified "words of power" as each was touched.

On November 12, 1988 I suddenly realized that the shape of the "chambers" in the chakras within the body is that of a pyramid. Also on this date began an interesting set of exchanges with another person. In mid-1988 I had happened to sit next to an interesting woman psychologist on the plane going from Los Angeles to Boston. We had talked all the way to Boston and had exchanged addresses because I had promised to send her some information. I had sent the information and assumed that would be the last of it. But, on November 12, **DK** suddenly said that this woman, whom I will call M—, and I were "one" or Soul Mates, many centuries and lives ago, in Atlantis! (Talk about an interesting statement!) I thought about this for a few days. Then, on November 22, I asked **DK**:

"Was the last time M— and I were together in Atlantis?"

DK: "Yes."

HK: "Were we physicians?" (I don't know why I would ask this question. It just popped out.)

DK: "Yes."

HK: "Did we operate together?"

DK: "Yes."

HK: "Were we lovers as well as physicians working together?"

DK: "Yes."

HK: "What kind of physicians?"

DK: "Scientific physicians."
HK: "Will we work together again?"
DK: "Yes."

(HK Note: After several months of subsequent correspondence and contact between us, M— decided "Not to participate" in **DK**'s work so it is now unlikely that further work will be initiated between us—at least during this lifetime, although I can still feel her soul within me whenever I wish!)

On November 13, 1988 I awoke about 1 AM and was told that I was now to receive energy. It came in three great waves. This energy simply flowed over and around and through me and became a part of me. Afterwards I was told that I now was given the energy of an Ascended Master which was "essentially infinite and which extended indefinitely in all directions." (Tap into this energy if you like by following earlier instructions.)

On December 2, 1988, the following came through:

"Turn off your electric blanket. You will never need heat again. You will not need the new down jacket you just bought."

(Nov.1991. This hasn't happened yet. I still need warm blankets and jackets.) I then "saw" lines and dots of light in different patterns as though my body was being rewired.

December 8, 1988: I flew to Denver for the beginning of a second Four Winds Foundation program called "Healing and Energy Techniques of Shamanism." This one was directed by Alberto Villoldo, the Four Winds Foundation leader and shaman. We drove from Denver to a Zen Buddhist retreat at Lindesfarne, among some of the American Indian's sacred mountains, south of Denver, for a three day weekend. Remarkable things happened on this trip. For instance, on the first morning there, at sunrise I found myself saluting the rising sun with arms outstretched and later on my knees praying to it without knowing why I was doing any of these things. Could I have been an American Indian in a past life? Later, one of the women of the group, when staring into my left eye, said she could see a very ancient and wrinkled indian beyond my present features. I did some very powerful and unexpected channeling for this same woman. I connected her to Pacha Mama by touching her forehead with my right hand and Pacha Mama with my left hand, as she lay, and I sat next to her on the ground. It was a wonderful and startling experience for both of us, as I suddenly began channeling The Christ, Pacha Mama and others for her.

December 15, 1988, 2AM: another strange statement:

"Within us (you and I) is placed the seed of growth to exceed that of other human leaders(?)"

(This last word was not clear)

On January 12, 1989 I channeled for one of the women at work, who was having personal problems. That night I received the following:

"This action is the beginning of your ministry on Earth. You are beginning to understand the energies which were given you and can now use them for the good of mankind. You are now at the stage where you can go beyond The Christ (Remember when He said, 'All the things which I do you can do and more"?). Healing by touch is now possible. You will be the modern day Merlin or Delphi Oracle or Indian shaman, except much clearer in your directions and skills. Get comfortable with these energies and use them wisely. You will become a national resource used in your government, and on loan to other governments, to help them solve their problems. With the help of another you will be healers of the psyche of whole countries, not so much of individuals, instilling confidence and efficiency in governments."

I am not going to comment on many of these statements because I was speechless when I first heard them and am still speechless four years later!

January 13, 1989, 2 AM: This morning **DK** said that the woman whom I channeled for yesterday and I have a strong bond between us. We had been married to each other and lived in Pompeii almost two thousand years ago, although in that life she was the male and I the female. We had three children together.

On January 16, 1989, at about 2 AM, while trying to open the third eye per **DK** instructions, I heard the following:

"This exercise is no longer necessary. The third eye will now gradually open by itself and reveal to you all its beauty. Have patience."

(I'm still waiting and still have patience (11/91).

On January 24, 1989, about 4 AM:

"Visualize yourself as a great and bright pillar of Holy Light, growing larger and brighter all the time."

On January 27, 1989, at about 4 AM I asked **DK** about my Kashmir message. He said:

"The 'You were one with another' statement in your experience in Kashmir referred to the Higher Self (which I prefer to the word Soul although they are the same). I (DK) and your Higher Self are essentially 'one.'"

On January 30, 1989 I made the following note: The home which I designed, and where my wife and I lived in New Hampshire for about 9 years (between 1981 and 1990), was a pyramid in shape, the roof being made up of four equilateral triangles. I typically would meditate in the third floor near the top of the pyramid. I slept either in the second floor, still within the pyramid, or in the underground portion of the house below the pyramid. On the noted date I asked **DK** if the shape of the house helped my spiritual development.

DK: "Yes."

HK: "Significantly?"

DK: "Yes."

HK: "Would the same thing have happened without the house shape?"

DK: "Yes, but much more slowly."

HK: "Is it OK to sell the house?"

DK: "Yes, but you must warn the new owners about its energy."

(This was done although I doubt if they believed me.)

On January 31, 1989 at about 5AM I asked **DK** the following "As my light increases in intensity, will others be able to see it?" He answered:

"Some will and some won't. You must get used to others coming to talk to you because of it."

(No one has yet done so by 2/93). On the same day , while meditating at work about noon, I suddenly saw (with my eyes closed), the brilliant and vibrant colors of a peacock's tail in my mind. Spectacular! The colors were as though the sun was shining on them and every color was literally glowing.

February 1, 1989, about 2 AM: Immediately after scratching my forehead at the site of the third eye (because it was itching) I was told:

"The third eye can send out a beam of energy which you must learn to direct and control and utilize. When you learn to do that, it will no longer be necessary to touch someone's forehead to heal or work with them."

February 5, 1989, 9:30 PM.

"Your light is now shining for many to see. Your chakras are now all one. It makes no difference which one you concentrate on. Your third eye is now beginning to function well, and you can now heal without touching."

(I don't notice anything different here yet, 11/91).

146

February 7, 1989, about 4:30 AM, While trying to Let my Light Shine, I began to feel a headache. **DK** says:

"All OK. You are starting to use new sections of the brain. There may be some discomfort but that is OK. Don't worry about it."

I began to feel an itching at the third eye again, and began mentally to move energy around at it, and to feel a ray coming out of it. I felt that I was starting to control the direction of this ray. **DK** then came in with the following interesting statement:

" While kissing is fine for the physical body, we ought to touch our third eyes (that is, our foreheads) together to integrate emotional, mental and spiritual energies between individuals."

The evening of the 7th I began mentally expanding my Holy Light outward to my immediate surroundings, then to the town, then to the state, then to North America, then to the western Hemisphere, then to the whole world. I suddenly felt at one with Pacha Mama. What a wonderful feeling! I stopped when **DK** came in and said:

"That is enough for today."

February 7, 1989, afternoon. I suddenly began standing much straighter at work. Actually stretching upwards.

February 7, 1989, 9 PM.

"You are a giant among men! Act like one!"

(This command didn't work. I still have trouble believing all this.)

February 12, 1989, 9 PM Third eye itching again. Is there anything I can do to help the process?

"No. Just let it happen and enjoy the process."

February 20, 1989, 4 AM. The whole body seems to be receiving a different kind of energy than before. It seems to be just vibrating all over. This happened twice, each time for one to two minutes, but can't tell for sure. **DK** says this will continue to happen from time to time. (This is the second type of energy I have received. The third type will be noted later. I can't explain what the difference is because I don't know, and **DK** isn't offering any comments on their difference.)

February 22, 1989, 4 AM. Awoke this morning knowing that I was now "free from the tyrany of sex." Apparently when **DK** says something happened it means that the seed has been planted but it may take many months or years for me to know for sure that the event or growth is completed.

February 23, 1989, 3 AM. Awoke feeling energy going around me—but a different kind of energy, a softer, quieter energy. While it was still surrounding me I was told:

"This is the energy of LOVE. This is the third kind of energy and the last gift you will receive. This ends your receiving period. Now you must learn to use these gifts for the good of all mankind."

This last energy was given to me in many waves or clouds. Perhaps six or seven. (You should be able to tap into this last gift).

February 24, 1989. In California for our second Four Winds meeting. This one in Death Valley, a place without a past human history (probably because the environment is so hostile no one wanted to live there).

February 25, 1989, just before sunrise, while meditating alone on top of a near-by hill.

"This is your Transfiguration. You are now complete. No further messages on your development are necessary!"

Some time after this statement about the Transfiguration, I asked **DK** for his comments as to what this meant. His answer was as follows:

"Several initiations will be referred to in this text. Such initiations are described quite fully in my first book with Alice A. Bailey"

(titled <u>Initiation, Human and Solar</u>, 1922, chapter IX, Lucis Publishing Co. P.O.Box 722, Cooper Station, NY,NY 10276).

"These initiations are spiritual initiations and refer to an expansion in consciousness which takes place over a period of time (typically over many life times) and which create individuals who are capable of assisting in the growth of mankind to an ever increasing amount.

"The initiations, as I described them in this book, are very briefly summarized here for those who don't wish to look them up to obtain their complete description.

"First initiation: Typically called 'The Birth of the Christ' within the individual. The control of the Ego (the Soul) over the physical body must have reached a high degree of attainment. The heart center is the one usually vivified, with the aim in view of the more effective controlling of the astral vehicle, and the rendering of greater service to humanity.

"Second initiation: Typically called 'The Baptism.' A long period of many incarnations may elapse before the control of the astral body is perfected, and the initiate is ready for the second initiation. The analogy is kept in an interesting way in the New Testament in the life of the initiate Jesus. Many years elapsed between the Birth and the Baptism, but the remaining three steps were taken in three years. Control of the astral body is demonstrated. The emotional body becomes pure and limpid and the lower nature is rapidly dying. The sacrifice and death of desire has been the goal of endeavor. The throat center (or chakra) is typically vivified.

"Third initiation: Typically called 'The Transfiguration.' The entire personality is flooded with light from above. Psychic faculties are stimulated by vivification of the head centers. The aim for all development is the awakening of the spiritual intuition; when this has been done, when the physical body is pure, the astral body stable and steady and the mental body controlled, then the initiate can safely wield and wisely use the psychic faculties for the helping of the race.

"Fourth initiation: Typically called 'The Crucifixion.' The life of one who takes the fourth initiation is usually one of great sacrifice and suffering and even esoterically is seen to be strenuous, hard and painful. All is renounced, friends, money, reputation, character, standing in the world, family, and even life itself.

"Fifth initiation: 'An Adept.' After the fifth initiation the person is perfected as far as this scheme goes, although it is possible to take two further initiations if desired. The force or energy of the planet (esoterically understood, and not merely the force or energy of the material planet) is at 'his' disposal.

"Students must get rid of the idea that if they are 'very good and altruistic' suddenly some day they will stand before the Great Lord. They are putting effect before cause. Goodness and altruism grow out of realization and service, and holiness of character is the outcome of those expansions of consciousness which a person brings about within themselves through strenuous effort and endeavor. Therefore it is here and now that a person can prepare themselves for initiation, and this they do, not dwelling upon the ceremonial aspect, as many do in excited anticipation, but by working systematically and enduringly at the steady development of the mental body, by the strenuous and arduous process of controlling the astral body so that it becomes responsive to three vibrations -

"1. That from the Ego or soul or higher self.

"2. That from the Master.

"3. That from 'his' 'brothers' everywhere around 'him' or 'her.'

"They become sensitive to the voice of their higher self, thus working off karma under the intelligent guidance of their own Ego. They become conscious, via the Ego, of the vibration emanating from their Master; They learn to 'feel' it more and more and to respond to it ever more fully; finally, they become increasingly sensitive to the joys and pains and sorrows of those they daily contact; they feel them to be their joys and pains and sorrows, and yet are not incapacitated by them."

(HK Note: With regard to this last comment, for several years now when ever I see an accident or even hear about pain, whether in real life, on the TV screen, or even someone just talking about it, I literally feel that pain in myself at the place it is occurring in the person. It can be quite painful and discomforting. Fortunately it doesn't last for long, just a few seconds. But I know it is going to occur when I see such a thing about to happen. I also now literally feel the emotions of others such as joy or sorrow. I have always wondered why this happens. The last sentence in **DK**'s statement above, which I had first read long ago and forgotten about, clearly states why I am subjected to these disconcerting occurrences. (11/91 input))

March 12, 1989. The last two days I have been told to put a particular quartz crystal on my forehead when in bed, and visualize myself as a pillar of holy light growing larger and brighter. (I had been doing this exercise whenever possible for the last week without the crystal). About 5 AM I was told:

"You can now travel anywhere in the world or universe when desired."

Last night I asked **DK** if he was in the mind of many others as well as myself. He said

"Yes."

I then asked "How many can you do this to?" He answered:

"An infinite number!"

For the last two or three months **DK**—through me—has been designing a most interesting desert house. I have not known why this is happening, just that I suddenly became interested in designing a new and strange house. The design is now essentially complete and **DK** says that a particular town in Arizona (that I have never heard of) would probably be the best place for it.

March 18, 1989: HK mentally to **DK**: "Over the last two or three weeks I feel strange, occasionally, as if something was happening, but it goes away and nothing seems to result. If I am complete why don't I know it?" **DK** answered;

"You are like a growing lotus. You are complete, so you can grow, but first roots must develop and shoots (below water level) appear and grow. It is only after leaves break the surface that you are sure something is happening, and not until a bud forms, and opens, do you know its full glory."

March 23, 1989: I began to feel energy tingling throughout my whole body again. I felt it all evening and the next evening. I found that I could initiate it by thinking of the word "Love" and sending love out to everyone and everything.

March 24, 1989: As I watched the movie <u>Golden Child</u> on TV, I was suddenly told that I was a "Golden Child," except that I had much more capability than was shown in the movie.

March 29, 1989:

"As you walk or sit, radiate divine light from the head and divine love from the heart."

April 1 and 2, 1989: I suddenly decided to give myself a birthday present by going to Sedona, Arizona, to visit some of the vortexes that I had read about there. After arriving in Phoenix I suddenly decided to drive to this little town **DK** had mentioned as a possible site for a new home, before going on to Sedona. On arriving there I decided to visit a real estate agent, and look at possible building sites. The first real estate agent didn't show me much of interest. But a chance meeting with a resident there sent me to a second real estate agent. One of the places he showed me was spectacular. Very strangely, this place had come on the market just 3 days before! When I asked **DK** if this was an interesting location, he said:

"This is the place. We can do good work together here."

The lot had already been offered to someone else, but they turned it down so I immediately made an offer, even though I hadn't planned to even look for a home site when I began this trip. (The offer was eventually accepted, **DK**'s home was built on it (just fitting the lot), I suddenly decided to retire, and my wife and I now live there!)

After visiting this town I drove on to Sedona. There I visited every vortex—14 of them. What a powerful place. The first vortex I visited turned out to be the most powerful one, called "The grandfather of us all" by the other vortexes. I was in it from before dawn to about 11 AM, meditating. As I left, I suddenly was able to converse with Pacha Mama, the vortexes, trees, rocks and animals. Very startling and totally unexpected! After leaving this first vortex I continued to the subsequent ones, each new one utilizing this new ability to communicate with me by telling me where to sit to meditate, how long to be there, and often telling me, as I was about to leave, that they had given me a gift as well. On one site—a wonderful, modern church on top of a vortex—the tears flowed for perhaps fifteen minutes. I asked the vortex why this one was so powerful. It said:

"Because here we combine the works of Man with the works of Nature, the two energies combining and flowing

together to produce a unique and special energy field which is available to all mankind to help them grow and understand."

April 25, 1989: For the past few months very often, when looking at a digital clock, the time would be three of the same numbers such as 333, 444, or 555. This occurred far, far more often than would be expected normally (statistically, one would expect such an occurrence about every 200 looks.) Here it was occurring at least once in ten looks, and sometimes once in three of four looks. Something is obviously happening. **DK** wouldn't clarify except to say that 5/5 (May 5) would be an important day for me. (Note: This occurrence of often seeing the same numbers is still happening to this day—2/93)

April 26—May 4, 1989. I have been sleeping with a quartz crystal that I seem to vibrate to. It is apparently helping me change so that I will be ready for a major shift on 5/5.

May 1, 1989. I awoke with the feeling that my "Love" and "light" energy points had now merged and I was now surrounded by one large, integrated field in the shape of an egg rather than by 3 smaller heart and head areas, or points.

May 2, 1989, 5:15PM. While driving home from work (from Lexington, MA to Salem, N.H., a distance of about 35 miles) I was suddenly told that, after the "shift," I would no longer be the sole inhabitor of this body. I must now share it with another! I was told that this other was to be my higher self and that we would, on 5/5, share knowledge, wisdom, and the physical form, each contributing their capability, neither totally in control. We would gradually merge. This was so startling and unexpected, in spite of all my study and reading, that I had to give a great deal of thought to this loss of control. I finally agreed (before getting home that night) because it would greatly increase my capacity to help others and the planet. I was told that I would begin to change physically (appearance) as well as mentally, but this would occur slowly. Now others would begin to see my light.

May 4, 1989, 5AM.

"This is the beginning of your Transformation weekend. During your last trip (to Death Valley) you went through the Transfiguration. On this trip (with the Four Winds group to Canyon de Chelly, AZ) you will be Transformed. Enjoy the process and remember it so you can write about it. You are the first to go through this. It will be exciting because you will learn, and become capable of, things you only dreamed about. Good Luck. The next time we speak you will know me differently and I will be one with you."

May 5, 1989, morning. Alberto, our shaman group leader (who had opened his third eye during his shaman training) and I roomed together last night in Albuquerque before leaving for Canyon de Chelly. This morning he told me that when he came into the room last night (about 10:30 PM—I was already asleep), he could see a hazy oriental figure, probably male, and clothed in a white robe, bending over me and working on my head. He said the energy level was so high in the room that it took almost an hour for it to dissipate so he could get to sleep.

May 5, 1989, morning. I was driving one of the vans to the canyon through the Navajo Indian reservation when I was stopped for speeding, even though others were going considerably faster than I was. The Navajo policeman completed the writing out of the ticket, and was about to hand it to me, when he suddenly changed his mind and gave me a warning instead. As we were driving away two of the women in the van told me that they had been sending him love energy, and felt that this was the reason he changed his mind.(**DK** says it was). Later I asked **DK** about this ticket. He said:

"This was a warning for you. You must now realize

that you can no longer consciously break any of man's laws. If they are not good laws you can work for their change, but you must now obey them. In the case of driving, because speedometers are inexact and it may be dangerous to others if you are restricting traffic you will be allowed to go up to 5 miles per hour over the speed limit, but no more."

May 5, 1989, afternoon. After driving to Canyon de Chelly we (Alberto, a Navajo guide, and the group of about 17 of us) began climbing down into the canyon. On the way down, the spirit of the Anasazi (The Ancient Ones) suddenly began talking to me saying:

"You and your group are welcome to our valley because your hearts are pure and your minds are clean."

On our second day in the canyon we spent most of the day hiking through the canyon in silence, ending up in a very steeply walled box canyon. **DK** said that there was more power closer to the canyon walls and I should have my head as close to the wall as possible. I therefore located my tent under a slight overhang so my head was exactly under the massive canyon wall. After our evening ceremony I walked back to my tent, passing Alberto on the way. The next morning he told me he saw much energy, and several spirit people, following me to the tent. As usual, I saw and felt nothing during the ceremony, during the walk back to the tent, and while sleeping. During our group meeting the next morning, each of us was asked to make any comments we would like. **DK** came through and I talked about how each of us was different with different characteristics and capabilities and none of us should evaluate ourselves or our abilities or progress by comparing ourselves to others.

I don't remember anything that might indicate that I went through a Transformation during any of the weekend. I did get to know M—better (one of the other members of the group and the one I had connected to Pacha Mama in the Colorado mountains), as we walked together for some distance. **DK** came through and told me to tell her that she would soon be going through the same transition that I was now going through, and she must also begin keeping a spiritual diary so others could know what she would be experiencing. It is important.

I also met H—on this trip. She just happened to be my seat companion on the long drive from Albuquerque and we got to know each other quite well. Both she and M—will figure prominently in something which happened many months later.

After leaving the group, I flew and drove to my new home site in Arizona. I slept there that night so I could begin to bond to the site. Early the next morning I noted a second hilltop adjacent to my site. On walking over to it, I was startled to be told (by the vortex) that there was a male, positive vortex on its top. (I had already found a female, negative vortex just on the edge of my new home location.) The male vortex then told me that it and the female vortex on my site were "married," and it was important that the two lots be owned by the same individual so there could be a free flow of energy between them. (Can you believe this?) I therefore drove down to the real estate agent, and finding that this second lot was still for sale, purchased it also.

May 11, 1989:

"During your last incarnation, you were Cochise, an Apache chieftain."

(HK note: After our move to Arizona, I found a place on the map called "Cochise Stronghold" where Cochise spent the last years of his life. We drove there and I spent perhaps a half hour or more trying to feel any of my previous energies that might still be around. No luck.) **DK** is saying as I write this:

"Don't be too surprised. Life energies do not stay in the

place of life or death. They move with the Soul for the development of the new lifeform!"

May 22, 1989, 1 AM:

"As of now your light can be seen by others and so you should expect comments on it occasionally. It will continue to grow stronger from now on and more will be able to see it as time progresses."

(Still no comments from anyone by 11/91)

June 17, 1989. I purchased two 17th century bronzes from a vendor at a local mineral show today. **DK** said after purchase:

"The small, bronze head of the Buddha was in a Buddhist monastery for more than a century and contains great power that we will use when we work together. The second bronze of the kundalini after rising is to be enjoyed for its beauty and delicacy, but contains little power."

June 22, 1989, 5 AM:

"All is going fine. When you are ready the change will occur. Have no fear."

June 23, 1989, 5 AM. On waking up, saw, in my mind, a light going from point to point, leaving a lighted path. **DK** says:

"This is the actual physical start of the change beginning to take place. While the cells were changed many months ago, now you will be aware of the changes taking place. Good Luck."

5:30 AM: Started to feel very nervous. **DK** says:

"Yes, this is all part of the change. Many strange things will happen from now on. They are all part of the change. Record them as they occur to act as guides for others who will be following you. Your light will now become visible to some others for the first time."

June 26, 1989, 8 PM. Strange feeling of sluggishness today at work. Very unusual. **DK** says:

"This is all part of the change. There will be many such strange feelings as the body prepares itself for its final form."

June 27, 1989, 10 PM. My brother, a doctor in Maryland, called to say that he has an advanced state of cancer and that it is inoperable. **DK** says I can heal him and to begin sending him light and love energies. On June 28, 1989 I sent him the following letter:

Dear B—,

I was, of course, shocked to hear of your sudden problem last night. However, as I told you last night, I am not quite the same brother you had a year ago. You asked for help or comments from the Tibetan. In the last year many things have happened based on, and apparently due to, my twenty year long search for wisdom and knowledge. In fact I am starting to think of writing a book detailing these very strange, and, at least to me, wonderful experiences.

In any case, let me simply say that I have become a channel for the Tibetan—and, in fact—much more than that because as I said to you last night we (i.e. The Tibetan or **DK** and I) have become one. This may sound very strange but I don't know how to describe it any better than that. We are literally one. If I have any questions of him, he is instantly there to answer me. He guides me constantly, telling me what to expect in the future, about past lives, how to handle situations, whom I can heal (yes, I have become a healer) and much, much more. More than I can describe because this already sounds like I have gone off the deep end. For instance he guided me to a piece of land in Arizona which I have since purchased and on which I hope to begin building a new home fairly shortly. He is helping me write this letter right now.

If you are still with me—and still believe that I am sane (I also have my doubts from time to time) as you were talking to me last night he was there with us and I channeled from him to you (when you asked "what was I reading from" during our conversation). Afterwards, I asked him if I could heal you. His answer was "Yes, he believed so." He used the word "believed" rather than just saying yes because in such instances, there are too many variables to be absolutely sure. Accordingly, I have begun sending you light and love each morning to begin the healing process. (He told me several months ago that I had now become powerful enough that I no longer had to touch the person requiring healing). He said that the healing process should be quite rapid with you and you should be able to tell the difference within weeks.

You must realize, however, that there is a fee for such healing. That fee is that you must begin to spend more time helping others. All of your life you have spent your energies and resources on yourself and your family. You must now significantly enlarge your area of interest and begin giving forth your unique capabilities to help others, and the Earth itself, to regain its health. No one will tell you how much of your time you must give. But you will know when you are being asked to help and you will know when you are doing all that you can to help. Opportunities for such help will begin coming your way. If you have any questions, listen to your conscience—your higher self. Begin to tune in on this wonderful, unknown part of yourself. It will never steer you incorrectly.

To help you with your healing process, I am sending you a small, crystal pyramid that I used to wear. To speed your healing process, wear the pyramid around your neck—on a small, gold chain—so that the apex of the pyramid is pointed in toward your lungs (where the cancer is). "Feel" the healing energy from it pouring out of the apex into your lungs. Later, after the healing is complete, turn it around so its energy is pointed out from you sending your energies out to help others.

I know that all of this may sound very strange, and, to a scientist, almost bizarre. I spent many months and years myself learning to live with these strange and wonderful things that I suddenly had thrust on me. For instance, I now—through mental telepathy—"talk" to plants, animals, and the Earth (Pacha Mama) itself—and I get back answers that are fascinating! And when I was in one of the most powerful places on Earth (Sedona, AZ) one of the major vortexes there told me that over thousands of years many had come there to talk to it. I was the first to listen to its answers.

If you are interested in learning more about channeling, you might read the paperback called <u>Channeling</u> by Jon Klimo. Another, but totally different, paperback is <u>Opening to Channel</u> by Roman and Packer.

Good Luck.

On July 14, 1989, at 6 AM, my brother's wife called to say that he had come down with pneumonia and was in the hospital and very sick but that the day before he looked much better. She now has high hopes for him. I continue to send him energy. After this call I suddenly felt my light burst forth into a full glow as though it was now free of me and had a life of its own.

On Sept. 2, 1989. **DK** told me that while I am now much more capable of healing, I must not yet send such new energies to my brother. He was still trying to digest the last batch of energy I sent him. This new, more powerful energy would be too much for him until he utilizes the energy already sent.

On Sept. 4, 1989, at 3PM, I received a call from my brother's wife stating that he had taken a turn for the worse after a new blood transfusion and wasn't expected to live through the night. With an OK from **DK** I sent him "total" energy, giving him so much that he should actually be glowing from it.

On Sept. 5, 1989, at 5 PM, I received a call telling me that he had passed away the day before about 6 PM. **DK** says that my brother gave up fighting at 4 PM. He says that once spiritual energy is sent to someone, chemicals in any form, even blood transfusions, will oppose each other and cancel each other out, leaving the body unprotected. He says that he didn't think the reaction would be as severe as it was, but the more spiritual energy that is used, apparently, the bigger the problem, and once the patient gives up then there is no more hope. Prior to this last problem, my brother had been doing fine. X-rays had shown that the cancer was getting smaller and his doctor told me at the funeral that he thought "he would beat it!"

On Sept. 5, 6, and 7, 1989, using the Tibetan Book of the Dead as a guide, I guided my brother's spirit across the Bardo (the "in between" plane of Tibetan Buddhism). We crossed safely together in three days. (This "trip" more typically takes up to 30 days.) I then bade him goodby and returned home.

Sept. 9, 1989, 3 AM. **DK** says:

"This is the first of your failures and you must get used to this because whenever human and spiritual energy are in conflict there must be 'winners' and 'losers' and because humans have the right of self-determination, if they cannot be swayed in their thinking or understanding, then they will 'win' and they will carry out their desires.

In order to keep this story complete and easy to follow, I listed it in its order of occurrence, omitting other things that were happening during this same period. The other story now continues:

July 1, 1989, 5AM. For several months now, but especially in the last two months or so, **DK** has told me that there is another great being in me, but no name was ever mentioned. I have tried to guess, but no further hint was given. This morning while reading A. A. Bailey's <u>From Bethlehem to Calvary</u>, page 142 I read "Christ, therefore, at the Transfiguration, unified in himself God and man,..." God is the new being in me! **DK** confirms this and says:

"Yes, of course, now you understand."

Months ago when I first began channeling, the voice kept saying and repeating "You are God" and similar expressions but I couldn't understand. It was like a broken record, saying the same thing over and over in different ways. But I kept dismissing it as being ridiculous. Now I know that this is real. God is literally a part of each of us!

July 2, 1989, 6 AM. For the last two months or so I have been using a particular crystal of quartz at night, communicating with it, following its directions and keeping it nearby when I slept. On awakening this morning I suddenly realized that my work with it is completed. No longer do I need to work with it. The crystal is now within me and a part of me!

7 PM: While watching a TV program on the Egyptian Pharaoh Akhenaten, **DK** came in saying that I had been Akhenaten!! (Nothing further on this until now as I write this (8/22/91) when he is saying:

"That was your first attempt to teach mankind about God. This present life will be your second attempt—and hopefully much more successful than the last."

(Historical foot note: From 1364 to 1347 BC Akhenaten (originally known as Amenophis (Amenhotep) IV) was Pharaoh of Egypt. During his reign he replaced the old religion of many gods with the worship of one god, represented pictorially by the sun with hands extending down from it as rays of sunlight.

The previous Egyptian religion was headed by the god Amun, together with other Theban gods who, during the New

Kingdom (from 1551 to 712 BC), had overshadowed previous deities. Because Akhenaten's original name included the name of Amun, he changed it to Akhenaten meaning "The solar disc is content."

During his reign he moved the capital of Egypt from Memphis to Akhetaten (now called Tel el-Amarna) where he built a totally new city. After his death there were political/religious problems, during which his new religion of monotheism, or worship of only one god, was abolished and the old religion of many gods reestablished. The capital was then also moved back to Memphis, and the magnificent new city of Akhetaten was wiped off the face of the Earth.

This change back to the old religion occurred during the leadership of his successor Tutankhamun (note the reintroduction of the word amun in his name) who ruled for just nine years—from 1347 to 1338 BC. Because of his youth, he was easily influenced by the old priesthood.

From 1338 until 1290 BC there were four Pharaohs. In 1290 Pharaoh Ramesses II ascended to the throne. Ramesses II has often been identified—without much evidence—as the Pharaoh who oppressed the Israelites. It is believed that Moses, who modified Judaism into the belief of one god, lived about 1300 BC. If this time is approximately correct, then as a child growing up in the Pharaoh's household (whichever one it was), he could have easily been exposed to the teaching of the one god by Akhenaten or one of his remaining followers. This basic concept could then have been modified, by him and those who followed, into the present monotheistic religions of Judaism, Christianity and finally Islam. As I write this, **DK** is saying:

"This is basically correct and Akhenaten wasn't a total failure in teaching of the one god, but almost all that he taught was lost."

July 4, 1989, 3 AM.

"Let your light shine. This is the third time I have told you this. Each time you have removed a veil. Now you must remove all the remaining veils so your light can blaze forth in its full glory."

July 25, 1989, 5AM. I realized that I am not to just let my light shine. The light is to extend out from me to all I meet or encounter or come near. It is to be like a cloud of light and Love that anyone near me is enveloped in and knows.

August 1, 1989, 4 PM.

"This will be a good month for you. Much good will happen."

August 2, 1989, 1 AM. Very strong energy input from about 9 PM until about 12 PM. Rereading A. A. Bailey's The Light of the Soul for the third or fourth time. Page 296 says "This light in the head is the great revealer, the great purifier, and the medium whereby the disciple fulfills the command of the Christ, "Let your light shine." And later on the same page, "Through this light we also become conscious of that which is hidden or as yet unrevealed. The Mysteries are revealed to the (one) whose light is shining and (they) become a knower."

August 8, 1989, 1:40 AM (Note the numbers again 8889).

"This day marks the beginning of a new life for you. Many things will begin to happen to you as you are given new gifts. Do not be concerned about strange things that may occur. Many of these gifts will be given a human for the first time and we aren't sure what will be the results. Grow, learn, try to understand. Utilize these gifts for the good of all mankind. Good Luck. You are to become the most powerful human being ever created. Many others are to follow. Each will be different with different gifts and capabilities. Go with God. Your light will now grow so intense that many who have never seen auras will see

yours. You will be able to transport yourself to anywhere in the universe at will—in any time period—and take others with you."

August 10, 1989. I left for San Francisco for the final meeting of our Four Winds group in the redwoods of Big Sur on the California coast.

August 17, 1989, 5:30 AM. So much has happened since last Thursday when I left for Big Sur that it is hard to remember or describe. First, on the long drive to Big Sur from San Francisco, M—and W—, another member of the group whom I knew only slightly, and I just happened to get in the same car together so we were alone for the full, several hour long drive. As we began the drive, I began channeling and was startled to find that all three of us were of great spiritual age, and had each been brought back at this time—and been brought together at this time—because of our particular abilities which would be needed in the future. Each of us is to write a book of our experiences in going through the initiations. Each book will be different as each of us views it, and will be for a different audience.

During our long hike up to our camping site, H—and I just happened to walk together for most of the distance. As we hiked higher and higher through the wonderful, tall redwoods, I could feel a great sadness about me and asked the redwoods why. They said that with the inception of the chain saw they were now being cut down at a much faster rate than they could grow and their time on Earth as a useful life energy was now limited! I also channeled for H—during this hike. She said she had just been offered an important job and I told her she would soon be offered an even more important one. This first job was just a preliminary step for her.

During a mix up in transportation, before the long hike up to the redwoods where we would camp, M—'s and my backpacks, with all our camping gear, were strangely lost, and left at the parking lot. We each had to sleep in other's tents, with borrowed blankets and extra clothes, since our sleeping bags were also below and it would be almost freezing at night. The first night I slept next to W—so I could transfer energy to him. The next night I slept next to M—so I could transfer energy to her as well. How I knew that this should be done, and how to do it I don't know. It just happened! There was no touching involved. Just the fact that I was within inches of them was all that was needed, along with my consciously sending energy to each. However, earlier that second night, I had also touched my forehead to M's forehead to transfer psychic energy to her. Again, I don't understand how I knew that this should be done. During that second night (I was told by **DK** the following morning—a Sunday) M—and I went through the fourth initiation together!

Early that Sunday morning I asked M— to accompany me to the nearby stream where I put some of the stream's water on both her and my forehead, baptizing us both. It was as though I was in a dream because I had no conscious idea that this should be done or why it was being done. I just knew that it was to be done. Following our baptism we went into a nearby circle of majestic redwoods and on our knees I prayed for us to be able to carry out our tasks. As I was doing this, the tears began to flow again, and I remember saying "with these tears I return to you, Pacha Mama, the water which you loaned us for this baptism."

August 14, 1989, 5:30 AM. After leaving Big Sur I flew back to Arizona to visit the new home site. I spent the night on the site and as I watched the rising sun the next morning I suddenly heard:

"You are offered the reigns of power as the most powerful being on Earth—to use all honest methods and

energies available to return this Earth to the reign of God and his assistants and to help Earth to return to the ways of God!"

What would you do if you heard such a message? First you would be pretty sure that you were crazy. Then you would say, OK, now that I am crazy, what do I do about it? Then, at least I, said "What the heck, if I'm crazy, I might as well go along with it and accept the challenge even if I haven't the vaguest idea what they're talking about. But I'm certainly not going to tell anyone about it!" (Not only are you the first to hear this, I had great trepidation about even putting it in here, but **DK** says:

"It is part of the story and must be included here."

But please don't automatically chuck this book for this reason alone. There are going to be even more reasons to chuck this later on so you might just as well read on and find out what these additional reasons are.

Two days after returning from Big Sur and my home site, my wife and I drove to Lake Champlain for a mini-vacation. On the way there, as we drove past forests and mountains and lakes, I thought I would test that last offering. So I mentally asked all of these for their assistance in this great task. They answered! And accepted willingly. And called me "Great One!" They then said:

"All the Earth is mobilizing to help with this very diffi-cult task!"

This story that started out so simply is getting stranger and stranger and I am having more problems believing it and writing about it!

I can occasionally see **DK** smiling as I now talk to him. I am trying to read up on the meaning of the fourth initiation but I am not finding much on it that I can understand.

August 20, 1989, midnight. I suddenly awoke with a feeling—no, knowing—that someone important had just died!

Unable to find out. I suddenly felt **DK** within and asked him if it was I who had just died. He replied:

"Yes, your material part. You have just passed through the fifth initiation and are now ready to begin your life's work. We wish you well."

August 23, 1989, 3:40 AM. I am now at peace. I have expunged my body of sin and karma and am ready to begin my great work. My light can now shine freely and unhindered.

August 24, 1989, 5:30 AM. To **DK**: "How will I know what gifts I have and how to use them?" He answered:

"You will know when they are needed and how to use them. While you are now compete, you will continue to grow in knowledge and understanding. When we are working together in Arizona you will begin to understand what you have become. Until then it will be difficult for you to comprehend these changes. Don't worry that you don't understand these things now. Your vehicle is now prepared and ready for them as needed. Allow energy to flow into and out of you freely."

September 2, 1989, 3 AM. I have been rereading **DK**'s A TREATISE ON WHITE MAGIC for perhaps the fourth or fifth time and am astounded at how much more I now understand it than in any of the previous readings. I now understand almost every word and sentence. As I'm writing this, the following just came through:

"It is now no longer necessary for you to say anything as you heal others. Simply assemble the energies necessary and direct their flow through out the body. You will now cause healing to occur at a much faster rate."

I tried sounding AUM silently and was startled at how much more powerful it was.

Another note from **DK**:

"We are well pleased with your progress to date. You

are one of the Christs that will be appearing on the Earth in physical form to help the Earth over this very difficult period. You are beginning to collect your disciples—as are others. You will become fully functional shortly."

September 22, 1989, 2 AM. At last I am free of doubt. I now know that one must have absolute and complete faith that growth and enlightenment are possible before they can occur. When The Christ said "He that believeth in me, all these things that I do, you can do and more," the key phrase is "He that believeth in me." Without total and complete belief and acceptance, the rest is impossible. After the belief, THEN comes the study and work to make it possible. That is step 2.

September 28, 1989, about 4 PM. At the Arizona home site, Debbie (one of the real estate sales persons that I bought the lot through) joined me at the property. She said she had seen me in a dream, with a body of light rather than as a person. When I then asked **DK** about this strange comment he confirmed it! He said:

"You are a being of light and energy rather than a human and were brought here eons ago to be activated at this time to help the Earth over its Great Transition which is about to happen. You have been going through many incarnations since arriving eons ago to become more human so that you would understand humanity and its problems. You are from a different, far away galaxy and have some gifts which are not available in our solar system but which are required for this Transition."

October 1, 1989, at work. I asked Marty, my chemist assistant, if he would conduct an experiment with me. He was to empty his mind and close his eyes and see if I could telepathically send him a picture of what I am, because I now don't know what I am.

Afterwards, he said all he saw was scattered bursts of light.

Which, I guess, is what I am? Driving home this evening Marty talked to **DK** for the first time and told him that I was an alien. **DK** then told him through having him write down letters one at a time that I should be referred to as a VISITOR. Marty then asked **DK** to overshadow him—as he had done once before when we were talking together about something that had recently happened to me—if all this was true. He told me the next morning that he was then overshadowed as he was driving down the road.

October 4, 1989. I came down with a bad cold, the first one in a long time, and was told by **DK** that I must not take any medicine, not even aspirin to relieve the severe headache. I must simply put up with it or I would have to go through it again. He said he was working on my astral body and needed a weakened body and mind to be successful. A very bad night. Got essentially no sleep. Entire head ached continuously and severely, nose running, etc.

October 11, 1989. In response to my question about the cold, **DK** said that the reason for the headache (or at least much of it) was that he had raised my kundalini "fire" from the base of the spine to the head or crown chakra. This does cause some pain which is why it was done in secret and partly hidden by the effects of the cold. When I told him I didn't feel any different, he said that these effects—like almost all spiritual effects—take time. When I then "opened up my thoughts" to having a raised kundalini energy, I felt a new prickling all over the body. This recurred every time I thought of the kundalini.

In answer to my question "What should I now do to help?" he said:

"You need to do nothing. The path is now open, the way is now clean. You will begin noting effects in the next few weeks and months. In effect, you are now totally complete and the great work can begin—very slowly at first—so we

CHAPTER 11

THE FORMATION OF THE GROUP
AND FINAL CONTACTS

It seems that each additional contact surprises me more—if such a thing is possible. However, the next contact really startled me because I suddenly was talking directly to God! Obviously I don't know how to do this, and yet here was a conversation which I seemed to be listening in on. Perhaps this was my Soul talking and I was just privileged to listen in? (Actually a new being was beginning to come through me and become a part of me and this was its initial contact with "us.")

October 11, 1989, 5 AM. The "new" HK—to God:

"Oh Great One, I have been brought through time and space to help you in this time of great change and need. I am now ready to be activated, to be of any service that you wish, and to serve as your instrument as needed."

October 12, 1989, midnight: I have been trying to have a water well drilled on the new home site in Arizona per **DK** instructions. On my last visit **DK** told me exactly where to drill the well and said:

"You will find water at about 152 feet."

No water at 155 feet, or 215 feet or 330 feet. I stopped the drilling at 330 feet at the suggestion of the driller (via telephone) and with an OK from **DK**. We will hook up to city water. When I questioned **DK** earlier in the day he said:

173

"Don't worry. All OK."

Tonight, after stopping the drilling and going to bed in some confusion because of the failure of **DK**'s prediction (and almost $7000 wasted) I questioned him about it. His answer was as follows:

"The new hole was not for water! You have two vortexes of energy on your property. These form two legs of a tripod of energy that you are to eventually manipulate. This new leg—really a hole—will form the third leg of that tripod for you. The two vortexes utilize energy from near or at the surface of the Earth. This new 'well' will provide energy from deep within the Earth—like a hypodermic needle draws blood from inside the individual out to the surface where it can be collected.

"If you draw a line connecting this energy source on the east side of the house with your feminine vortex on the west side of the house (The house by DK direction is exactly square and oriented precisely north, south, east, and west—true—not magnetic.) it would run through the center of your KIVA and under the glass pyramid."

(HK note: Needless to say, this house that **DK** designed is not an ordinary house. A large (16 foot diameter) North American Indian KIVA, made of adobe brick is in the center of the house. Over it is an even larger glass pyramid (twenty feet by twenty feet). The whole house was built in the ground on a rock foundation after about two to four feet of existing rock was jack hammered out of it, and then soil built up around the house so the house is essentially two thirds buried in the ground and thus part of the Earth.)

A few months ago, long after we moved into the house, **DK** told me that the KIVA concentrates energy from the Earth, while a pyramid concentrates energy from space or the heavens. Because the pyramid is precisely over the KIVA, the two types of energy meet in the space in between, and create a new kind of energy which is neither positive nor negative, male nor female. It is simply pure energy, the first time such energy has been created on Earth. Now, to continue **DK**'s comments,

"I didn't tell you about all this at first because it was just too complicated."

October 21, 1989, 7:30AM. In the shower—HK 3 just appeared!

(HK note: I've taken to calling my "original/physical" self HK 1 and my Soul/**DK** HK 2. HK 3 is the body of light and energy from the other part of the universe.) My mind feels strange and HK 3 says that he is starting to take over. I told him that he is welcome to take over but he says HK 1 and 2 and God will not disappear. We will share the same space and I, as well as **DK** and God will be astounded at what we are capable of.

I asked him how I should refer to him and it said it would prefer "it." I then asked if it would begin sharing in hours, days, or months. It said:

"Days, not months."

The sharing began immediately and I had a strange feeling in the head for several seconds. I have had the same feeling for the past two or three months, but more softly and gently. I knew that something was going on, but not what. Now I don't have to wonder if it was just my imagination.

October 22, 1989, 8 AM. Feeling HK 3 much stronger now. I asked it why this didn't take place while I was sleeping and it said it must take place during the conscious state. It says we will share the body, not displacing HK 1 and 2, and likes the term sharing.

October 23, 1989, 5 AM. While trying to mentally help myself to glow, suddenly found myself expanding until I filled all of space everywhere. That is, I was everywhere, out in space and on the Earth.

October 24, 1989. In spite of comments on October 22, I felt the change beginning in earnest last night. Many dreams of changing to light. Perhaps the actual change takes place during the day and I become aware of it while sleeping? (**DK** says:

"That is much too simplistic. It is a very complicated process which is going on, something like shoehorning two or three giant super computers together into one small cabinet with their millions and millions of connections which have to be integrated into one. This process is still continuing even after two years! HK 3 has been there all along. It has just been watching and observing all this time—and in all the previous lives as well. This is its first chance in thousands of years to come out and get ready to express itself. No one knows quite what to expect."

(11/91 input)

October 31, 1989: Very powerful dream and thoughts on waking.

"Send a message to all humanity about stopping the killing of animals, cutting of trees, catching fish, and selling of drugs. All must be told to stop such action and find new occupations. All with wealth must begin helping others instead of wasting funds on luxuries. All must begin to prepare for the coming world crisis."

I was "overshadowed" by **DK** for the first time to let me know that he was aware of—and directing—my thoughts during this statement.

November 5, 1989, 6AM: While reading a book on Egypt to my wife she asked me "why the move to Arizona?" **DK** came through and began talking about how important the new home in Arizona was—how we (**DK/HK**) would be wandering through the universe, how we would control the forces of Earth—wind, snow, storms, rain, and much more—all over the

Earth from there. My wife then asked if we would be wandering in the physical body?

DK said:

"The body is unimportant—we will be wandering with our 'spirit.'"

(HK note: My wife doesn't believe any of this, so asking such questions was very unusual for her. These answers didn't help any!)

November 7, 1989, 5 AM. While meditating in bed this morning and working on "Letting my light shine," I received the following:

"With this touch I bring to you, and to all within hearing distance who wish to hear, the clear white light of God and the pure golden light of Love to help you help others, to help you grow spiritually, and to help you help yourself.

(DK note: "This prayer is to be used by all those who believe in God and who wish to help others to do so. It should be done with the receiver on their knees (with their eyes closed and mentally picturing the energies described coming in through their forehead and spreading through out their body), and the giver standing and touching the receiver's forehead.")

I also learned the following—if asked the question "Are you a priest?" The answer should be:

"If you mean, 'Am I a servant of God,' the answer is Yes. Yet I serve no particular religion—only that great entity that most of you call God. I try to communicate with him when necessary and carry out his bidding.

DK Note: "The terms 'him' and 'his' are used here for convenience and do not imply that God is male. God has no sex!"

November 10, 1989, 8-9PM. **DK** wrote the following letter (through me) to three individuals (two women and one man—

the three individuals mentioned previously in my recent spiritual trips) and extended to them an invitation to join me to help restore the Earth during the next ten tumultuous years:

"Dear M—, W—, and H—,

"This may seem like a very strange letter to you—or you may have been expecting it. I don't know. Part of this letter will be from DK, and part from HK as DK wishes.

"We are now about to begin the last decade of this century. As some of us know, this will be a very difficult decade—the worst from a natural disaster standpoint in the last 6000 years. The four of us are being asked by the Spiritual Hierarchy to act as their emissaries on Earth during this period. We will become much like The Christ or The Buddha was in their time—to instruct and guide humanity through these difficulties. Each of us will be 'activated' as our bodies become fit for the energies that the Hierarchy will begin pouring in and through us. HK first, then M—, then W—, then H—. The focal point for the four of you will be the home we are currently building for HK in—, Arizona. This home will have a very high spiritual energy level, and will be HK's home, but will be available to all of you—and your spouses if you wish—for meditation and contact as you wish.

"M— and W— are already somewhat aware of this information. I am asking you H—, in this letter, to join us so that we are a balanced group, two women and two men. I would also like to ask your husband to become the chronicler of the group and especially to chronicle your changes as they occur in you so that a complete record of the changes which occur are known to mankind. This was not well documented in either the life of Jesus or The Buddha and has resulted in many problems and misunderstandings for us. HK has been documenting these changes for twenty years. M— and W— have now begun documenting them. The combined documents of you four, together with the changes that will begin occurring in each of you and in the Earth over the next decade will become the 'Bible' of future centuries. We thus hope that your husband will accept this vital task and understand its importance to the growth and understanding of humanity in the future. He can, of course, write anything else about what will be happening that he wishes, for his or others uses.

"Each of you must understand that we will provide all of the assistance that we can to help you carry out your vital tasks. Each of you has been chosen with great care— with your different backgrounds, cultures, educations, knowledge, and capabilities. Each of you will be given what you will consider to be true God-like capabilities. You will be guided and taught how to utilize these, and will then be free to use them as you see fit. We will always be available to each of you as you require and as you request. Your powers will be worldwide and you will work throughout the world.

"Enclosed are two sets of literature that we believe will be of interest to you. One of these, in particular, should be very valuable to you because it indicates to some extent what the world was like, shortly after the last major Earth change some 6000 years ago.

"HK's—and your—home in Arizona should be completed in about four months and we hope that all of you—and your spouses if you wish—can meet there some time shortly after that. The KIVA in the center of the house will allow all of you to truly become one as each of you— separately and together—becomes aware of and begins your great work.

"We wish you well and earnestly hope that all of you will accept this truly great challenge which will set the 'tone' for millennia to come."
DK

The following are excerpts, sometimes with slight modifications for clarity, of the letters that followed:

Thanksgiving Day, 1989.
Dear H—,
Thank you for your letter of Nov. 14. I hope you don't mind but I am sending a copy of your letter and this response to M— and W—, as well as to you, because even though I haven't heard from them, I'm sure they are having some of the same thoughts you described so well.

If you think you are the only one having problems with what **DK** wrote, think again. I didn't know what I was writing you until it was there in black and white, and even then I couldn't quite be sure what was said, and have read and reread that letter perhaps a hundred times since then! And I have been slowly prepared for this for more than a year! Remember, you were trained to work with people and human variations. I am a chemical engineer and was trained to work with things. I have been a scientist for more than forty years. I have been a director of research and technical director of major companies, and president of an engineering consulting company for more years than I care to remember. I work with facts, with hard knowledge that can be proven and rechecked by others. Yet with this background, more than twenty years ago I began studying **DK**'s books because "I had to." Since then I have traveled the Earth, studying religions, people, cultures—always trying to understand what people and cultures are, why they are as they are, what the Earth is, etc, etc. Yet, strangely enough, as I now write this, I know that I didn't really know why I was doing it. I just knew that I was driven to seek out "something." I also knew that I was tested again and again, although at the time I just thought some very strange occurrences were happening.

Many of the "things" which occurred in the past to me have been nothing compared to what has happened in the last year or so. Let me enumerate a few of them from my diary. Let me warn you, however, that this may be to my detriment since you might then "know" that I am "crazy," but you asked in your letter "what does activated entail?" so I am selecting a few of the items that may partially help you understand what has been happening to me lately. Realize, however, that we each are unique and your development may be quite different from mine since I must be considered a "difficult case," always questioning everything that happened, and then weeks or months later again repeating the same question to be sure I remembered it correctly and wanting to know how this all fitted together, and what was the purpose of it all. OK, with that background, take a deep breath and lets begin.

(Six pages of selected portions of my spiritual diary then followed)

Well, H—, there you have just a small part of it, warts and all. And this was in answer to only one of your questions! Why you? **DK** says "it is obvious." How is that for an answer? Several of your next questions were answered in the diary. **DK** and Alice Bailey were not the same. She was a channel for him as am I. Concerning your husband's question of what sort of Earth changes are in store, **DK** says:

"Changes so far reaching that you can't imagine them. Drastic climate changes, shifting of the Earth's axis, huge earthquakes and storms, huge volcanic eruptions, massive destruction and death everywhere."

What are my unconscious motives? **DK** says I'm too dumb

to have any!

How do you like that answer?

Why has this invitation been extended to your husband? Because he is competent, capable of understanding, and married to you, and therefore available to watch and listen to you. What will the group do in Arizona? I haven't the vaguest idea. **DK** says the home site will probably become the most holy place on Earth when we are all there and even he is not sure what will happen. But it will be exciting, he says. Concerning your questions on alcoholism etc, he says there is no single answer, but the work we will be doing, starting in Arizona, will begin the process of healing the planet and the people on it. It is impossible for him to give a more acceptable answer at this time.

I plan to retire and permanently relocate to Arizona "when the time is right." I don't know what this means! (**DK** is laughing at me over my perplexity at that answer of his.) This morning I plan to go to my local book store and pick up a book on Akhanaten that they ordered for me so I can try not to repeat the mistakes he made this time! I asked **DK** the other day if I was being given a second chance and he told me I was.

December 10, 1989

Dear M—, W—, and H—,

It has now been one month since I first wrote you three about **DK**'s and the Spiritual Hierarchy's request for our assistance. Since then I have received two telephone calls from W— saying he is having problems with his ego, one telephone call from M— telling me she just got back from a trip and two letters from H— asking me impossible questions like what does "activated" entail and telling me I have a Messiah complex. So it has been a wild month for me also.

Nobody has said "I have faith in God and lets give it a try!"

What have the four of us been doing for the last ten to forty years if it hasn't been to try to prepare ourselves for just such an undertaking? Each one of us has traveled throughout the world, taken weird and wonderful courses, gone to places no one in their right mind would go to, and in general done nothing more fitting than prepare ourselves for just such a request as we have now received. We are all totally different and yet totally the same in our continual spiritual striving, in our ability to look at the unknown and try to make sense of it—at least to ourselves. H— said that I have a classic symptom of megalomania etc. How else do you think I could have even written that letter to you if I hadn't been told all those things by **DK** over a period of time so that I came to believe that at least some of it was possible? A "stupid" engineer asking a psychologist, a lawyer, and a housewife to follow me to Arizona? How much crazier can you get? Especially since I've only known each of you for only a few days?

Actually I was so disappointed in your answers that I asked **DK** to forget the whole thing. His comment was:

"It is too big a job for one person to do!"

What had I expected for an answer? The following: "You're crazy, the job is crazy, but so am I—Lets do it!"

H— asked me "what is entailed?" How do I know? If what **DK** is asking is true, only a few people in the last six thousand years have gone through it and none of them wrote about it! H— further says she will not become a disciple to anyone. Who asked her to? All I was told was that we each would be given God-like abilities and taught how to use them and would then be free to use them as we see fit. Where did it say we had to be a disciple to anyone? This is still as new to me as to you! **DK** did say I was beginning to collect my disciples. Somebody has to collect someone. With all the free spirits around these days, if nobody collected anything, somehow, nothing would ever get done. As you can see from my spelling from the diary, I didn't even know how to spell the word disciple!

If you look up the meaning of the word disciple in the dictionary, it means "the follower of a teacher or school." If it makes you feel any better, consider God the teacher or consider the school the school of hard knocks!

Well, I've said enough, I think. I'm now at a stage where I don't really care if you decide to join me or not. But please give me the courtesy of telling me what your decision is. Just write me a one line letter which says

1) Let's go for it or

2) It's too wild for me, maybe next time.

Christmas Day, 1989

Dear M—, W— and H—,

First, M—, let me thank you for the two tapes, one by another channeler of **DK**, and your long letter. Even my wife enjoyed the tapes! And I especially enjoyed **DK**'s comment on enlightenment vs delusion in his tape. After H—'s last letter I wasn't sure whether it was enlightenment or delusion. However after **DK**'s tape which said:

"It is a very fine line between the two but if you continually ask questions about it it is enlightenment."

I feel much better because I'm a real and continuous asker of questions, even if I'm not satisfied with the answers, as H— wasn't in my second letter.

Well, nobody has yet said "Lets forget the whole thing" so I guess all is not lost, although I haven't anyone saying "Lets go for it " either. I guess a request of that kind takes a great deal of thought. So let me know of your decision when you can. Someone did say that they have an alternative for me, if someone decides to drop out, so I guess that is positive, although **DK** wasn't particularly thrilled with the idea of not getting all of his choices. He says that he really did select each of us with the greatest of care!

Apparently he has been watching and WORKING WITH EACH OF US for many life times, not just this one. He says that , therefore, he can't just add someone to a partial group and expect to get the same results.

The real reason for this letter is because while I was trying to decide what I could do or say to each of you that might help me sway your thinking (this at 2 AM this morning) I went back to my favorite book, the one book that I have worked with for twenty years, and which I must have read or listened to at least a thousand times, because I read it onto a tape and have listened to it while I drove to and from work every day for many years, almost every time learning or understanding something new from it. Its title is simply <u>Light on the Path</u> and it was first printed one hundred years ago in 1888. The author is listed as M.C. or Mabel Collins but **DK** says it was channeled from the Ascended Master Hilarion. In any case, early this morning, I suddenly started reading it again and was startled by how much more I was understanding it than ever before. I, therefore, decided to send each of you a few excerpts from it that I thought might help you with your decision.

I Finding the Path

These rules are written for all disciples: Attend you to them.

Before the eyes can see, they must be incapable of tears.

Before the ear can hear, it must have lost its sensitiveness.

Before the voice can speak in the presence of the Masters, it must have lost the power to wound.

Before the soul can stand in the presence of the Masters, its feet must be washed in the blood of the heart.

Grow as the flower grows, unconsciously, but eagerly anxious to open its soul to the air.

Each man is to himself absolutely the way, the truth and the life. But he is only so when he grasps the whole individuality firmly, and by the force of his spiritual will, recognizes this individuality as not himself, but that thing which he has with pain created for his own use, and by means of which he proposes, as his growth slowly develops his intelligence, to reach to that life beyond individuality. When he knows that for this his wonderful separate life exists, then indeed and then only, he is upon the way.

(HK note: Especially for you, H—, and as **DK** explained to M— in her last telephone call to me, these books all talk about "he" because until you two, all previous disciples in this latest "go around" have been male. That is the reason he is so unsure about how we will work out as a team. We will be the first "team" and the first with women in it. All previously have been individuals and very few women, and those a long, long time ago.)

But not until the whole personality of the man is dissolved and melted—not until it is held by the divine fragment which has created it, as a mere subject for grave experimentation and experience—not until the whole nature has yielded self, can the bloom open. And in the deep silence the mysterious event will occur which will prove that the way has been found. Call it by what name you will, it is a voice that speaks where there is none to speak—it is a messenger that comes, a messenger without form or substance; for it is the flower of the soul that has opened. It cannot be described by any metaphor. But it can be felt after, looked for, and desired, even amid the raging of the storm.

II Treading the Path

Having obtained the use of the inner senses, having conquered the desires of the outer senses, having conquered the desires of the individual soul, and having obtained knowledge, prepare now, O disciple to enter upon the way in reality. The path is found: make yourself ready to tread it.

Inquire of the earth, the air, and the water, of the secrets they hold for you. The development of your inner senses will enable you to do this.

The knowledge which is yours is only yours because your soul has become one with all pure souls and with the inmost.

It is a trust vested in you by the Most High. Betray it, misuse your knowledge, or neglect it, and it is possible even now for you to fall from the high estate you have attained.

III Notes

When after ages of struggle and many victories the final battle is won, the final secret demanded, then you are prepared for a further path. When the final secret of this great lesson is told, in it is opened the mystery of a new way—a path which leads out of human experience, and which is utterly beyond human perception or imagination.

Remember, O disciple, that great though the gulf may be between the good man and the sinner, it is greater between the good man and the man who has attained knowledge; it is immeasurable between the good man and the one on the threshold of divinity.

—try to lift a little of the heavy Karma of the world; give your aid to the few strong hands that hold back the powers of darkness from obtaining complete victory. Then do you enter into a partnership of joy, which brings indeed terrible toil and profound sadness, but also a great and ever increasing delight.

Know, O disciple, that those who have passed through the silence and felt its peace and retained its strength, they long that you shall pass through it also.

To be able to stand is to have confidence; to be able to hear is to have opened the doors to the soul; to be able to see is to have obtained perception; to be able to speak is to have attained the power of helping others; to have conquered desire is to have learned how to use and control the self; to have attained self-knowledge is to have retreated to the inner fortress from whence the personal man can be viewed with impartiality; to have seen the soul in its bloom is to have obtained a momentary glimpse in thyself of the transfiguration which shall eventually make thee more than man; to recognize is to achieve the great task of gazing upon the blazing light without dropping the eyes and falling back in terror, as though from some ghastly phantom.

It is true that in every civilization the star rises, and the man confesses, with more or less of folly and confusion, that he knows himself to be. But most often he denies it, and in being a materialist becomes that strange thing, a being which cannot see its own light, a thing of life which will not live, an astral animal which has eyes, and ears, and speech, and power, yet will use none of these gifts.

The disciple is compelled to become his own master before he adventures on this perilous path, and attempts to face those beings who live and work in the astral world, and whom we call masters, because of their great knowledge and their ability to control not only themselves but the forces around them.

—and by the force of its internal vitality steps over the threshold into the place of peace. Then the vibration of life loses its power of tyranny. The sensitive nature must suffer still; but the soul has freed itself and stands aloof, guiding the life towards its greatness. Those who are the subjects of Time and go slowly through its paces, live on through a long-drawn series of sensations, and suffer a constant mingling of pleasure and pain. They do not dare to take the self in a steady grasp and conquer it, so becoming divine; but prefer to go on fretting through divers experiences, suffering blows from the opposing forces.

"With faith, all things are possible." The skeptical laugh at faith and pride themselves on its absence from their own minds. The truth is that faith is a great engine, an enormous power, which can accomplish all things. For it is the covenant or engagement between man's divine part and his lesser self. The use of this engine is quite necessary in order to obtain intuitive knowledge; for unless a man believes such knowledge exists within himself how can he claim and use it?

To have acquired the astral senses of sight and hearing; or in other words to have attained perception and opened the door to the soul, are gigantic tasks and may take the sacrifice of many successive incarnations. And yet, when the will has reached its strength, the whole miracle may be worked in a second of time. Then is the disciple a servant of Time no longer.

Well, it goes on and on. If you are interested in reading it further, please let me know and I will make copies of the whole text for you, since I am unable to find copies of it in bookstores anymore.

December 29, 1989
Dear M—,
You mentioned blocks to your channeling **DK**. I think we covered that in your telephone call. However, **DK** would like to make a few additional comments:

"I had the same problem with HK when he first started to channel. He says he could actually feel the fear rising up within him. What you must do is simply relax and know that all will be all right. Nothing can happen to you through

channeling because you are a conscious channel and can always stop or ignore the communication if it doesn't 'feel right' to you. All you have to do is want me to come through, then ask me to do so and then relax. It might be slow at first, as it was with HK, but as we begin to work more and more together it will get easier. We have much to do together in the future so the sooner, the better.

"Concerning your question about visualization, this will occur after we are much closer together and have channeled for some time. It will occur when we are ready and need it.

"Concerning your 'line of communication' to your higher self, STOP WORRYING. You are doing fine. All these things will happen when they are needed, not when you want them to happen. You are already way ahead of HK from an age standpoint as to when things are beginning to happen. Of course your soul participated in the design of humanity's ascension process. It is very active now and will bring you up to speed when you are ready."

Concerning your soul ray and your personal ray, **DK** says they are unimportant at this time.

"Leave them be—they will have essentially no effect on your future progress and can only confuse you as you move ahead. In this case too much information is bad for you. You are so much like HK that it is hard to believe it. You want to get ahead, but when it starts to happen you're afraid of it and question yourself as to whether it is really happening. It is HAPPENING and we will see that you have all the information you need when you need it. In the meantime, relax and read <u>Light on the Path</u> that HK will very shortly be sending you. You both continue searching and that is fine. But don't try so hard! Read any books you want but don't search so hard for their meaning to you.

Feel their message rather than try to intellectualize it. The previous book on Egypt that HK sent you was to help you see the quiet, relaxed, searching and simple type of life rather than for you to get any very specific messages about anything."

Concerning your questions about integrating the different aspects of self (such as my HK 1, 2 and 3), **DK** says:

"Enjoy them—they are all different and all the same. You will have a like menagerie before too long. But yours will be different and in some cases even more exciting. However, it will be a little easier for you because you are at least aware that such things happen. With HK, it was totally new—and none of my books talked about such things."

(HK note: As you see **DK** now comes in and out of me pretty much at will and sometimes I'm not sure who is talking—but it is always interesting to read what I have just typed!)

January 12, 1990
Dear M—, W— and H—,

"We are one! Everyone has agreed to become part of this unique experiment in world history—to grow and expand our abilities and consciousness and weave them together into one all-powerful unit which will be capable of actions undreamed of by humanity!"

(Obviously **DK** is writing this!)

DK is saying:

"And so, now the work begins. Each of you can read M—'s letter in which I describe how to allow me to begin coming through you. Try it if you feel ready. If not, don't push. (And all readers of this book can also try this technique, It will work for you also if you are also ready) It will begin when you are comfortable and have prepared your-

self mentally for it. This will be 'The Voice of the Silence' described in the book <u>Light on the Path</u>.

"As I establish closer contact with each of you, you will begin establishing closer contact between yourselves. As you feel more comfortable with me, we will begin pouring specific and precise energies through you to permit you to grow and to gradually learn what you are in the process of becoming. There is no danger involved. However, because you are the first group ever to go through this, we are not sure exactly what you—as a group—will become. But it will be wonderful to behold—in what ever direction 'it' decides to go. Simply allow this to happen. You will know if it is 'right' for each of you and together as a unity. If you decide you do not like or wish it to go in that direction, simply mentally stop it and change its direction or stop progress entirely that way. Any 'one' can stop all movement in any direction. You can have a joint meeting and decide together whether you wish to continue in any direction or not. However, you all must agree to progress or there will be no movement in that direction. I hope this answers M—'s comments in her letter and H—'s unwritten questions.

"As we grow closer—and more powerful—you will begin to more thoroughly understand the abilities that we are being given and the good that we can do—both on Earth and elsewhere.

"I cannot discuss more at this time except to let you all know that we ourselves are watching this expansion of human consciousness with the greatest of interest and anticipation.

"Go with God!"

DK

February 16, 1990
Dear M—, W—, and H—,
DK says:

"**All is moving forward well and you are all beginning to accept what we have been talking about. There is nothing in particular that any of you must do at the moment except enjoy the literature that HK is sending you. It will give you a better understanding of the general things that we will be concerned about in the immediate future. Allow the energy that I am beginning to send each of you to flow through and around you and become part of you. You will become more sensitive to this energy in the next few months as I gradually increase its intensity and breadth. Know that we are beginning to watch and work with each of you more intensely now and as you begin to channel me, your knowledge of these energies will become more known to you.**"

"**Go with God.**"

March 23, 1990
Dear M—, W—, and H—,

I would like to suggest that we plan to meet in Arizona on the day of the Gemini full moon (Friday, June 8, 1990) or as soon thereafter as possible.

H— asked some time ago what we would do there. I am just beginning to find out. The purpose of the get together is primarily to simply get together at the home site. Nothing specific must be done. We will begin to bond to each other, and to the site, and together begin to gather and utilize the spiritual energy that is there for our use.

Both M— and H— mentioned going to Sedona before coming here. **DK** is saying:

"**Be careful there. Do not spend more than three days**

there and preferably not more than two days there. It is a **very powerful energy center and your newly developing energy cells could be overstimulated and permanently harmed with too much exposure. Enjoy it—it is a spectacular place—but do not become enamored of it. It is not for any of you."**

March 31, 1990
Dear H—, W—, and M—,

I thought you might be interested in a comment that **DK** made at work on March 27. I was doing some channeling for my chemist assistant at work when **DK** suddenly came out with the following:

"The four of you are the prototypes for the future generations of humans, that is, the next step up in human development. The difference between you, that is, your abilities, and current humans will be much greater than the difference between Cro-Magnon Man and present day Homo sapiens!"

April 11, 1990
Dear M—, W— and H—,

Concerning your comment, H—, that **DK** isn't talking to you yet, he says "cool it." All is under control and you are getting more from him than you realize. You should begin knowing him very soon. (HK note: From my experience this could mean a week, a month, or several years. Time doesn't seem to mean the same to the Masters as it does to us. When I think of very soon, it usually means hours or at the most days). He says you will be one of his most powerful pupils.

Hang in there. **DK** says:

"All is going ahead beautifully. We are right on schedule, if anything a little ahead of it."

He will continue working with each of us right up until the June summit, after which we will start to more control our own destiny. However, he and others will remain with us to guide and help as required and requested.

April 27, 1990
Dear M—, W— and H—,

Enclosed is a copy of Rule Four of **DK** on sound, light and vibration from his <u>A TREATISE ON WHITE MAGIC</u>. As I reread it I found so much that might be helpful to us all that I had to send each of you a copy.

I have also enclosed a copy of H—'s recent letter so you could read of her experience in 1981 of "a sudden light in the head."

W— called on April 23 to mention that he had been attending a course on healing recently and suddenly found that he knew all that was being taught even though he hadn't heard or read it elsewhere. As I write this **DK** is saying that W— will be our supreme healer. All of us will be able to heal but W— will be exceptional at it.

I just ran across a book called <u>Unknown Man</u>. It talks about the development of the next new species of man. As I read it, I could then more easily accept what **DK** had said in my March 31 letter about our being the prototypes for the next step up in human development and I could feel things begin to happen within me. This has continued since then—for at least two days now. **DK** is saying that when you receive a copy of this book that I am sending you, please read it as soon as you can because it will affect each of you the same way it is effecting me and make our work in Arizona easier and more productive.

May 3, 1990
Dear M—, W—, and H—,

The latest input from **DK**/HK 2 and HK 3 (probably their most startling statement yet—and there have been some pretty startling statements up until now!):

"When you wish to become one with God you are to go into the center of the KIVA. In it is the most powerful vortex ever created on Earth. It is neither male nor female, neither positive nor negative. It is simply pure energy. It is oneness! As the group will become one in it."

May 25, 1990
Dear M—, W—, and H—,

This will be my last letter before we meet in Arizona on June 7 for our "at-oneing." The house will be empty of things (i.e. unnecessary items such as pieces of furniture) but with all systems up and running including carpets and drapes. We have a front door now, so can enter the home properly although there won't be any landscaping, other than some of the original native plants that were saved as carefully as possible along the entry (purification) path. (HK note: The garage is located almost 200 feet away from the house. Close to the garage is an eight foot high redwood Japanese style gate and fence. The purpose of this gate and fence is to symbolically close off the house from the outside world. As one goes through the gate, one is supposed to give up the cares of the world and concentrate on and prepare oneself for the spiritual world as represented by the house. Hence the name "purification path.")

Enclosed is some final input from **DK** in case you have time to read it in the next few days. It is his Rule Five on "The Soul and its Thought Forms" from <u>A TREATISE ON WHITE MAGIC</u> and is one of the most important chapters in all of his books. As you will note, almost every line is underlined or otherwise marked by me as I read it at one time or another over the past twenty years.

July 2, 1990

Dear M—, W—, and H—,

Everyone is curious to hear **DK**'s comments on our meeting (so would I) so lets hear what he has to say:

"**All went well. All those things that were supposed to happen did happen. The group has now been formed and will begin to operate as a team from now on although none of you will be aware of it for quite some time yet. The KIVA is fully functioning now, and as W— mentioned to HK, it was 'activated' by the presence of all of you there at once.**

"**I think each of you wants to know what happened to each of you. You all want proof that something really did happen. I can't describe the many things that happened to each of you—individually and together—because such descriptions would have little meaning to you with your present knowledge and ability to interpret symbols and colors. Each of you will have to bear with me a little longer until your sensors are more fully developed and are able to communicate with you directly. Then you will begin to understand what I am talking about. Until then, please be assured that all is going well—and according to plan. The next few months will be 'quiet' times for each of you— except HK who will be moving into his new home very shortly and will then immediately begin to feel and work with the energies that will become one with him.**

"**Each of you should continue with your life as you wish and require. I will be in touch with each of you in the future as you continue to develop and grow in oneness—with me and with each other. HK will be very busy for the next few months and there probably won't be a need for him to contact you for many months, although we will be working** together and watching each of you, and helping each to develop as your particular soul dictates. Please feel free to contact us if you wish. And, of course, contact each other whenever you feel like it. You might tentatively think of getting together at one of the Spring full moons next year if you all can make it at once. If not, and you are in the area of Arizona, or simply wish to meet again for any reason—or no reason at all—please feel free to drop in.

"Thank you for spending the time, money and effort to make this last meeting possible. The results were beyond your wildest dreams, even if you realize none of it. Go with God."

This is HK speaking: I know this doesn't answer any of your questions but it is the best he would do for now. As **DK** mentioned, the move is now very close and we are packing like crazy. From then on I haven't the vaguest idea what will be happening.

Thank you for attending our first summit. I enjoyed it thoroughly. It was a great pleasure to begin to know each of you better. Each of us seems to believe it was worthwhile, so it must have been.

Until we meet again.

I will now go back to my diary which was continuing during the time of the group formation.

November 12, 1989, 4 PM. While walking on my 16 acres of land in New Hampshire, I was suddenly invited to go to the small vortex on top of one of my hills (I hadn't realized that there was a vortex there until this invitation). There I was given a special gift from all of the vortexes that I had visited in the last year or two. (I haven't any idea what this gift is. I just knew that there was a transfer of energy while there). That evening, the seventeenth century bronze head that I have suddenly began communicating with me and told me that this was a very special gift and I would learn about what it was in the coming months. (No awareness of this yet (6/92)).

November 13, 1989, 2:30 AM. I suddenly realized that the temptation that I went through about a week ago to tell **DK** that I insisted on going through the 6th initiation—so I would be greater than he—before I would cooperate—was truly a temptation of the devil—as Christ went through on the mountain top. At that time I realized what was happening—blaming it on my ego—and ordered the thought and desire to go away and telling the ego that I would not stand for such thoughts and desires in me. I now asked **DK** if this interpretation was correct and he said:

"Yes"

I then asked him who is The Devil? He said:

"Your lower self!"

(HK note: Isn't that an interesting statement?) He further clarifies this by stating that:

"Of course, your lower self isn't just the Devil but it is a small component which can come out and exercise great force if allowed to do so!"

As I apologized to **DK** for these thoughts, he said:

**"It is all right. You must go through these temptations, and this one you had to go through before we could offer you the leadership of the group you are now forming.'
'You are already greater than I—but different as well— because you are from another star system."**

November 14, 1989, 4 PM. While driving home from work, I suddenly realized (after reading portions of a channeled novel on Egypt the night before) that when I have been trying to "let my light shine," I have been doing it incorrectly. I have been trying to let my light shine so others could see it. Rather, I should let it shine so it will go out to—and help—others to become illuminated too.

November 23, 1989, 7 AM (Thanksgiving Day). Intense feelings of change, beginning about 6 PM last night, until going to bed. Began again on waking up this morning and continuing while I write a letter to one of **DK**'s selected associates.

November 28, 1989, 8:30 PM. Strong and continuing tingling over whole body, starting about 6 PM.

November 29, 1989, 1 AM. Awoke and immediately felt HK 3 continuing to merge. Don't seem to require as much sleep as previously. Tested again yesterday with thoughts that I couldn't work with **DK** because he is a Tibetan rather than a white. Stopped thought immediately and again apologized to **DK**.

November 31, 1989, 12:30 AM.

"This is an important day for you because beginning now, if you accept the energies now flooding into you, there can be no turning back. HK's 1, 2, and 3 will become permanent. Realize that you are the first for such a union and we aren't quite sure what will happen. Enjoy the new power which will result. Use it wisely.

"Concerning the abortion issue, The Pro Life forces are wrong. The soul does not enter the babies body until just before birth, NOT at conception."

December 2, 1989. In New York City with my wife, she to shop and just enjoy her favorite city. I, from what I was told the next day, to gain energy. On December 3, **DK**/HK 3 says I have now topped my batteries and gained enough energy to last through out the rest of my life. There will be no further need to go to NYC or any other place of energy input although he says I will go to such places often. While passing the UN buildings, **DK** said:

"You will address this body one day in the not too distant future."

(HK note: I mentioned this last comment in one of my letters to the group and H— wrote back asking me what I would say? My answer was "I would like to know what I would say." **DK** then came in saying:

"Don't worry. It will be from the combination of all of us and all of you and will be spectacular, shocking, and vitalizing"

(Whatever that word means (HK)).

December 4, 1989, 10 AM. I suddenly (at work) felt slightly dizzy. HK 3 says:

"All OK. I just pushed too hard. Good progress over the last few days."

December 5, 1989, 4:50 AM. Awoke full of joy and hope this morning. Know that things are going well and I will succeed in my task!

December 6, 1989, 3 AM:

"You leave on March 25, 1990 for Arizona."

(HK note: **DK** was too optimistic by exactly four months. We actually left on July 25, 1990. Maybe there were too many people involved to get accurate information? **DK** says that four months is a mere twinkle of the eye as far as he is concerned!)

7-8 PM. Very strong energy input from HK 3.

December 10, 1989, 4 PM. Believe my ability to heal has been greatly enhanced. Felt the palms of my hands being activated as I watched TV. **DK** concurs.

December 15, 1989. M— called last night and we had a long conversation. Even though none of the group has agreed to join, early this morning I suddenly felt M—'s spirit and mine start the process of becoming one. Very strange! Then W— and H—'s spirits also came in and the same process continued with them.

December 18, 1989, 9 PM. A really startling thing just happened! I just had a two way conversation with God! I can't remember anything that was said, but I'm absolutely sure it took place. It was too real to be a dream! How strange that I can't remember any of the specifics?

December 19, 1989, 4 AM. As the Christ I began sending Light and Love and Peace energies throughout the world! (HK Note: What is going on here? Nothing like this has happened before? Is this the result of the Christ energy coming through me or becoming part of me?) **DK** says:

"Both."

December 26, 1989, 8 PM. W— called to say that he accepts **DK**'s invitation to join the group.

January 8, 1990. I received agreement from H— and tentative agreement from M— to form the group. We have **DK**'s group!

January 9, 1990, 1 AM. Strange dreams about group oneness of ourselves, i.e. switching thoughts and actions between ourselves.

January 16, 1990, 5 AM:

"Your light is now shining continuously in all directions. Help it to do so when ever you think of it."

January 25, 1990, 4 AM:

"Now use the term 'Light and Love and Purpose' (instead of Light and Love and Power) in your meditations. The change is because you now have Power. What is now needed is the Purpose of to help others."

January 26, 1990. 2 AM. Awoke with my skin feeling activated or separately alive.

January 28, 1990. 5 PM. While watching the movie <u>Gandhi</u> on TV I asked **DK** "Will I be competent enough to carry out your (our) tasks?" **DK** answered:

"You will be competent enough. You have been trained

for this for centuries!"

January 31, 1990, 5 AM:

"You are the only one who is complete. The other three are still growing and learning and will be for several years yet."

Felt energy throughout my body for about 25 minutes before arising.

February 2, 1990, 6 AM. Very strange. While dreaming, golden light and energy was brought to me, then was radiated out through me into space. This happened over and over—perhaps 20 or 30 times. A wonderful feeling. (The reader should be able to experience this and contribute to the sending of such energy into space by following the directions in the Introduction. Be confident and relaxed and know you can do it! Try this as often as necessary until you experience it. This is important for you and the planet!)

February 7, 1990, 3 AM. Visualized clearly and precisely for the first time (perhaps the second time if you include the seeing of the peacock's tail several months ago). I saw the top of a Hindu temple in great detail and clarity—bathed in dappled sunlight. It was as though I was actually there it was so clear and sharp. I also began to visualize my light or aura as shaped more like my 17th century bronze statue of the kundalini (which shows it much like a flame instead of a circle) except that it begins more at the base of the spine instead of near the heart as in the statue.

February 8, 1990, 12:15 AM (Leaving for Arizona at 4 AM):

"Today you will know me more intimately than any man has known another as our fusion continues in Arizona. Today also you will be given gifts that are unique in Earth's history. This will be the gift of LIGHT."

(I am still not conscious of either of these 11/91).

February 22, 1990, 7 AM, While driving to work. Saw the sun rising just over the horizon and began sending love and light to it. Suddenly I was again hearing from the sun:

"You are the first in thousands of years to send me energy instead of me sending you energy. We are now truly one—twin suns."

February 23, 1990, 5 PM. Very strong energy input—the strongest yet. Also had similar input last night about 5 PM.

March 6, 1990, 8:30 PM. W— called to say he has been feeling energy input and his ability to diagnose patient's problems has recently expanded greatly because of his new ability to visualize the chakras of his patients.

March 15, 1990, 12:30 AM.

"The development of the four of you is like that of the butterfly. As humans you are like a caterpillar. As you are given various gifts you go through a stage like the caterpillar in its cocoon. Nothing is visible from the outside but you are changing internally and psychically. When the growth of the gift is complete you suddenly emerge with that capability—like the emerging butterfly. This corresponds to the previous example of a plant growing and the bloom opening but may be more understandable and acceptable as to what is happening within you.

"This is why the ancient Egyptians were prepared as mummies—to simulate the stage between the caterpillar and the butterfly—except that they weren't ready yet for the final emergence. This final stage is only now possible—and eventually possible for the whole human race. Thus your symbol should be that of a butterfly."

March 19, 1990, 9 PM. Returned from Arizona last night. Excellent trip. **DK** says much happened there although I feel nothing. Last night woke up knowing that the new house should be called "Spirit House."

April 5, 1990, 1:11 AM.

"With my arms outstretched I give benediction and supplication to all present instead of expressing agony as the previous Christ is depicted as doing."

(HK Note: This is the most powerful statement yet. Imagine yourself doing and saying such a thing! I was the one doing this, not **DK**! I'm still astounded at this statement more than a year later. However, as mentioned earlier, this is simply the result of the Christ Energy flowing through me. I'm also not sure what "supplication" means. I've looked it up in a dictionary but still don't fully understand its implication here. (6/92 comment))

April 7, 1990. To Arizona for the Easter full moon. Slept in sleeping bag in the partially completed KIVA.

April 10, 1990. Back from Arizona. **DK** says much good happened there but I feel nothing—as usual.

April 12, 1990, 9 PM. Very strong tingling over whole body. Lasting until going to sleep about 10:30.

April 26, 1990, 5-7 PM. Yesterday afternoon I started reading the book Unknown Man, The Mysterious Birth of a New Species. Strange feelings since then—like eating something sour and your mouth kind of squishes up—except this is occurring over the entire body and has been going on since last evening.

For the last 1 to 2 weeks I have had the compulsion to sleep with my iron meteorite—either with it on my forehead, in my hand, under my pillow, or just near me?

May 2-6, 1990. I have been having some pain in my right kidney area, making it difficult to sit or sleep well. Little input from **DK** except to mention not to worry and no need to see a doctor. Now (May 6, 8 AM) **DK** and HK's are saying this pain is part of the new growth process and it will eventually get less and then disappear. (HK note: This occurred as predicted, all pain disappearing in about a month.)

May 10, 1990, 12:20 AM. In Arizona, in the almost completed house, sleeping in the KIVA for the Taurus full moon/ Wesak Festival):

"There is but one GOD in all the universe, not a GOD in each planetary or star system. The KIVA is the best 'church' or structure ever designed to work with the energies of the Earth and to help heal it (and the people who are a part of it)."

May 30, 1990, 1:40 AM.

"I, as the Christ on Earth, send forth Light and Enlightenment, Love and Loving, Peace and Non-Violence to all Earth and nearby Space to help calm and quiet and expand mankind's thinking and abilities to understand and know me."

June 1, 1990, 10 AM: While walking in the woods at home, twice, each time for perhaps a second, felt my consciousness "shift" as though I was in another world or dimension or something? This is the first time I have noticed such a shift.

June 6-10, 1990, Gemini full moon/Christ Festival and World Invocation Day, Arizona: The group of four of us, two men and two women, from around the United States, had our first get-together. Very obvious changes in M— and W— during the meeting. Nothing obvious in H— or myself.

June 20, 1990. Strong feelings of change today, the first in some time.

June 21, 1990.

"You must learn to live with man, not hide from him."

(HK note: This was probably due to my making some comment about I'd rather be alone than in a crowd, or why, for the last two houses, they have been some distance away from other houses.

June 29, 1990, 1:30 AM.

"You must now begin to prepare yourself for the energy that will shortly begin descending into you. This preparation will be in the form of clarification in thinking and action. More quiet times. More feelings of energy input. This will be in a fairly continuous rather than a spurt basis. Invite this energy to descend into you."

July 12, 1990, 7:30 AM.

"Allow your light to flow forth from you so that all people may know it and be aware of it and become one with it."

July 25, 1990. Left New Hampshire for Arizona for the last time.

August 7, 1990. The workmen installed four large wood carvings on the new house and gate. A butterfly on the gate, a whale and a bird, one on each side of the entry door, and a full sun on the east wall of the house, facing the rising sun. The bird and the whale represent the air and the water respectively— two of the four ancient elements. The entry door was previously carved with a sun and a plant on it symbolizing fire and earth, the remaining two ancient elements. On installation, **DK** says:

"With these additions, the house is now complete and its work can begin."

One more note: I found that I prefer to sleep in the KIVA rather than in a bedroom for some reason. (And I am still doing this after almost a year and a half of living here)

August 31, 1990, 7 AM. I awoke several times this morning feeling that I was giving off light. When asked if this was the start of the physical change, **DK** said:

"Yes, now it starts."

October 10, 1990. Very strange day. My wife and I stopped in, unexpectedly, at an Indian arts store in Tucson. I immediately began feeling strange energies around some of the old Indian objects in the store—for the first time. I found myself suddenly giving energy to—and becoming one with—the lady proprietor of the store when I touched her forehead. This energy started her healing processes in her hands, ear and spine. The energy which I gave her seemed to concentrate in her ear—although she said her heart was also effected—and her left ear suddenly began to bleed immediately after the energy transfer. I seemed to know what to do and how to do it during the treatment, even if I didn't understand any of it.

November 5, 1990, 6:40AM:

"Your purpose is to teach, guide, help in understanding, giving wisdom, knowledge and ability. All is happening as it should. Do not be concerned on the slowness of your transformation. Much is happening."

November 10, 1990, 2:30 PM: While standing on the male vortex and facing the sun:

"The four of us (Sun, Earth, vortex, HK) are now one in our effort to return the Earth to the control of God and away from the destructive forces of man."

5:15 PM.

"DK and God will act as advisors"

November 24, 1990, 5:30-8 PM. Intense feelings of change through out whole body.

December 10, 1990, 10:15 PM:

"The time is now close for you to emerge from your cocoon of human life into your birthright of a star being. All is going well. Good Luck. DK"

December 11, 1990, 7 AM. Awoke sending peace and Love to the world.

December 19, 1990, 1 PM. The star Aldebaran in the constellation of Taurus, which includes the Pleiades, seems to be of unusual importance to me. Nothing more specific than that.

7:30 PM. While watching the Nutcracker ballet on TV, suddenly saw myself watching it with a different perspective,—as though I wasn't of the Earth but was an outsider, studying human response?

HK to **DK**: "Will I recognize myself when the process is completed?"

"Yes, but just barely."

December 25, 1990, 6:30 AM. High energy input and feeling of nearness of completion.

January 2, 1991, 8 AM. Very vivid and lasting dream that I opened a cage or a box and let a large, thick, furry butterfly fly out and watched it clumsily flap its wings to a nearby tree branch.

January 14, 1991, 4:30 AM.

"It is done. All the changes are made. Now you have but to wait."

January 16, 1991, 6:40 AM.

"The time of emergence is now very close."

January 19, 1991, 7:30 AM. Very strange. I woke up realizing that as one grows spiritually, the sexual urge gradually shifts to a desire to become one with your own soul rather than with another person. That is why the sexual urge continues and may even intensify rather than diminish as one would think. Until this is realized there is a great feeling of guilt associated with what are believed to be sexual desires. Therefore one should allow these feelings to flow through you rather than actively fighting them. Just channel them toward unifying with the soul rather than with another individual.

January 19, 1991, 9 PM. Very strong energy input most of day and evening.

January 25, 1991, 3:30 AM:

"You are to become the most powerful human ever created on Earth."

209

6:30 AM: "Will I know how to use it?"

"Oh, yes, that comes with it."

February 24, 1991, 2 PM. While channeling for H— who was visiting, **DK** said:

"Because rocks/crystals 'live' for so long, souls will enter them to learn and grow, then when they need additional experience, the soul will leave and other souls will enter and inhabit the structure."

March 1, 1991, 3:40 AM. Strong energy input. "It is beginning?"

"Yes, but it will be much more gradual than you expected."

In attempting to help the world solve some of its more serious problems **DK** will occasionally make suggestions of possible solutions. The following letter which was sent as indicated is one such suggestion:

March 14, 1991

The Hon. James A. Baker III, Secretary of State

Department of State

2201 C. St. N.W.

Washington, D.C.

Dear Mr. Baker:

I would like to propose a totally new type of solution to the Palestinian homeland problem.

FIRST, everyone concerned agrees that the Palestinians must have a home land.

SECOND, any thinking person must also agree that for one very small country to give up all the land necessary to create a practical new state is absurd, especially when ALL the lands in the area have changed boundaries for thousands of years and ALL are currently supporting large quantities of Palestinians— either with land or money or both.

THIRD, I propose that EACH COUNTRY IN CONTACT WITH ISRAEL—AS WELL AS ISRAEL ITSELF—DONATE A FIXED SMALL PERCENTAGE (AND ALL THE SAME PERCENTAGE) OF ITS OWN LAND AREA TO FORM A NEW STATE OF PALESTINE. Thus no one country is giving up an unreasonable and harmful percentage of its land area.

If we select this percentage as 1% of each country's current land area we end up with the following results:

STATE	APPROX AREA, (SQ. MILES)	1% OF AREA, (SQ. MILES)
ISRAEL	8,000	80
EGYPT	400,000	4,000
SAUDI ARABIA	850,000	8,500
SYRIA	70,000	700
LEBANON	3,000	30
JORDAN	35,000	350
		13,660

A country of 13,000 square miles should be a very reasonable size for such a new state—and would be many times larger than if it were all taken from only one small country.

FOURTH, that the areas to be donated be selected by the donor states BUT that there be no more than three resulting areas and preferably no more than two areas—connected by corridors consisting of a roadway plus some land on either side so a free flow of Palestinians citizens is possible.

FIFTH, three possible areas for such sites are 1) the area where Egypt, the Gaza Strip and Israel meet, 2) the area where Egypt, Israel, Jordan and Saudi Arabia meet, and 3) the area where Lebanon, Israel, Jordan and Syria meet.

If I can be of any assistance to you regarding this SIMPLE and FAIR solution please let me know.

(Copies were sent to the Israeli Ambassador to the US, and to the U.N. Secretary General. HK signed the note. No answers were ever received from anyone).

March 24, 1991, 7:30 PM. Very high energy input.

March 27, 1991, 3 AM:

"Begin expanding the light in your head so it includes the whole body."

April 16, 1991, 6 AM. Awoke knowing that after weeks of trying I had now unified all my body and brain cells into one large cell that can perform feats that are unknown to mankind. **DK** says:

"Now it can begin."

I have been working to accomplish this both while conscious and while sleeping. Mostly at night when the body is still and quiet.

April 18, 1991, 6 AM. Awoke feeling my body glowing.

"This light—which will gradually grow stronger—is known as 'The Fire of God,'" said DK.

April 25, 1991, 9 PM:

"You will need the new computer and telescope for some of your work. You will run the computer with your mind."

(HK Note: In the last few months I had purchased a new, powerful computer and a larger telescope.)

May 6, 1991, 10 PM:

"Let the light burst forth! Become a living ball of fire!"

May 15, 1991, 8 PM. Off and on headaches all day. **DK** says:

"No problem. Part of process. All OK."

June 21, 1991, 3:20 AM.

"As the body advances spiritually, the 'spirit' world becomes more visible to the entity."

July 24, 1991, 9 PM. Developed a fairly severe headache above the eyes. Very unusual for me. **DK** says:

"All OK. Part of change."

Headache still there about 2 AM on awakening. Mostly gone at 7 AM.

July 24, 1991, 4 AM:

"This is a gently world. We must learn gently in it. We push and strive too hard and all we get is disharmony and problems. There is enough for everyone and everything here if we don't try to take more than our share. If we would act more gently to the Earth, it would act more gently to us."

August 8, 1991, 10:30 PM. Very strong energy input. Whole body vibrating. I am mentally trying to help HK 2 and 3 plus **DK** and God to expand in body. First major rain storm in three months. I could literally feel the trees slurping up the water.

August 11, 1991, 9 AM. While walking in the outlying areas with some friends we met a lady on horseback. I tried to pet the horse's nose but he shied away. I mentally asked him why? He said (mentally) "You are different from the others."

August 12, 1991, 4 AM: From **DK**:

"We cleared a major blockage last night which was holding us back. Completion should be rapid now."

August 13-17, 1991. Very strong feelings of change—as though it is almost done.

August 18, 1991:

"You will wake up one morning in the very near future and know that you are now complete—and yet won't feel any different."

September 2, 1991, 4:30 AM:

"The time has come to reveal yourself through words and deeds."

September 6, 1991,3 AM. The last 2-3 days I have felt the change rate increasing again and lasting longer—especially in late afternoons and evenings but some during the day also. Have started to eat less, almost stopping the evening meal. Now feel "all squished up" as the change continues.

I suddenly received the following from The Christ

"I am wondering how the leaders of the Catholic and Protestant churches in North Ireland—and their superiors—can live with themselves. They should be considered criminals for permitting the warfare between them to continue and not taking a much more active role in stopping it. They have betrayed my trust in them!"

(I, as gently as possible, suggested that perhaps this would not be a very diplomatic statement to put in this book. However, I was told that such statements are necessary to shake up the present churches and remind them of their duties!)

September 9, 1991, 6 AM (Sunrise). Feelings of change now and for the past day more intense than ever. It is happening during the day, during evenings, during dreams, and immediately on waking up. (Continuing through September 9),

September 14, 1991, 2 AM. From Pacha Mama to all inhabitants of the Earth:

"You must win my trust again. And this will take centuries! You have raped and pillaged my surface and my air until there is nothing but disaster. Now I will fight back and it will not be pretty. You think you are in control. Little do you know that I have been waiting for you to come to your senses. But I can wait no longer and will now begin to act—as you have acted!"

September 16, 1991, 7 AM. Suddenly began physically

merging with HK 2 (My Soul). Don't understand this because I thought this had happened a long time ago but **DK** says:

"No, it only happened mentally, not physically."

I keep trying to get into the fetal position to make it easier. The Soul says this convergence does not include the head yet, only the rest of the body. My body is vibrating like crazy.

September 28, 1991, 11:30 PM. I am startled awake with the following command from **DK:**

"QUICK! Send out all the Light you have and follow that with as much Love as you can gather. You are being attacked by the gathered forces of evil!" (Some time later): **"You could have died! We will not be caught this way again! They attacked before we were aware of their gathering together! All is OK now. You are safe. In the future, be prepared to send out Light and Love as soon as you are aware of an attack."**

(HK note: I have a headache and am shaking like a leaf as I write this down and get ready to go back to bed.)

September 29, 1991, 5:30 AM:

"A very important thing happened last night. You had a brush with death but also a brush with infinity and because of that you were changed forever. Your abilities were expanded tremendously by that new contact. No one here knows what that will mean."

Oct. 20, 1991, 5:30 AM:

"If you are in a room or meeting with others, allow the twin energies of Light and Love to go out from you so that a true consensus—good for all—will emerge."

Nov. 22, 1991, 9 AM. Received the final chapter of the book from the Spiritual Hierarchy. (Chapter 14)

Jan. 1, 1992, 3:15 AM:

HK 2 and 3 to God.

"Oh, Great One, I am finally ready to begin my great

work. There was a slight delay as obstructions in me were cleared but now the Great Work can begin."

(During this transmission, my body was vibrating in a very unusual but pleasant way.)

May 13, 1992. Back from a trip to Mexico with a small group. Bad trip. Unable to spend significant time at Casas Grande ancient indian ruins because group leader, after promising to spend time there, decided that he would rather see other places. **DK** says:

"It was a hard lesson for you, but you had to learn it. Don't Trust Anybody!"

June 2, 1992, 7 AM:

"The process of completing all of your millions of hook-ups is still continuing to this day—and will have to continue for some time longer. It is taking much longer than expected. Having never done this before we had no idea of its complexity. All previous ones we did this to were much easier because not nearly as much was required of them!"

June 12, 1992, 7 PM: I was asked a question by a literary agent about the antichrist. **DK**'s comments were as follows:

"There is no antichrist as such. This is simply a convenient way of describing the evil in the world. By personifying it we can more easily grasp the problem— which remains with each of us, not with some ancient mythical character who we can blame for our own transgressions."

June 28, 1992, 4:44 AM:

"Let my Light go forth to correct human failings and to help them grow and understand and help others."

Summer, 1992. I have begun work developing a new kind of sailboat, one combining the technologies of aircraft, sailboats, kayaks, catamarans, and sailboards. It is being designed to operate primarily in the zone between water and air rather than mostly in either one (somewhat like a large sailboard but more controllable and stable). As work progressed, I was suddenly told that I was developing such a craft because it was necessary for me to learn more about, and begin to understand and "become one with," the two ancient elements of water and air. As can be seen, by not telling me the reason why I suddenly became interested in this rather strange project, I maintained my right of self-determination since I could easily accept or reject it and, if accepted, do anything I wanted with it before being told why it would be desirable. All of my trips were similar presentations as was the house and lot. (The boat should begin its first careful trials about June, 1993. 2/93 input)

December, 1992

Dear H—, M—, and W—,

This is the time of year **DK** usually contacts all of us at once to let us know what to expect for the coming year. Let's see what he has to say this year.

"Greetings. It is a pleasure to contact all of you at once and let each of you know that all is going as expected. You each are eager to get started on your final development and yet, none of you are really fully prepared yet for such a final effort. HK needs more time to realize what he is becoming and we need more time to help him with the physical/psychic changes that have been in progress for more than two years now. H— is doing fine. Her run for an elected legal position was very worth while and it matured her a great deal. Now she must begin spending more time looking within and doing the exercises that I have been sending her recently (through HK). M—, what a pleasure to have your address again."

(She divorced, remarried, and moved to a place where, strangely, HK's mother grew up and HK spent a summer on

217

his grandfather's ranch as a young child).

"We all missed your input and energy and thoughtfulness. Please let us know of any questions that you would like answered or any help that you would like to have. You have been going through a turbulent time and you really haven't spent the desired quiet time on yourself that is so needed for your continued growth. Don't forget all you have learned in the past because everything you do from now on will be building on it. W— is also finally settling down now that he has moved to the West. He is also doing fine although he still has much doubt about us. Every now and then, W—, you remember our input and suddenly see things happening that you don't understand and wonder if I have something to do with it. We are doing it together. Neither one is alone. I offer suggestions without you realizing it and you think they are your ideas. But that is all right. That is how we work. Never directing, only suggesting. You also need more quiet time in which you simply stop doing what ever you are doing and just sit, close your eyes, and look inside your self. Not much time is involved and you will find it very worth while and time well spent.

"As a group your ties are growing tighter even though none of you realize it. The bond that you formed both before and at (—, AZ) are permanent and can only grow stronger. They can never be weakened. However, none of you are consciously aware of them and won't be for some time. Your present lives don't require them yet so they are not yet manifesting in anything that you can grasp. Each of you needs to keep on studying, thinking, planning and growing. Two of you are now in California. Not a particularly steady or solid place. If you have the opportunity you might consider moving to a nearby state where the ground is not so sensitive to tectonic plate movement. On the other hand, such a move isn't required for some time.

"Please continue thinking about our group and try to keep as close in touch as you can. One day, in the not to distant future, we will all be together again and all much more developed and aware than at our first meeting.

"Go with God."

DK

January 4, 1993, 7AM. My cousin in California, who has been ill with Parkinson's Disease for several years, essentially unable to move herself or speak, had a heart attack two evenings ago (her daughter informed me). Now, suddenly, as I arise, I am flooded with pure joy and she says:

"It is so wonderful to be free of that confining and cold body. All is OK."

On calling her husband a few hours later he said she had been declared brain dead and all treatment was stopped about that time.

January 22, 1993. A different—and seemingly coarser—type of energy began flooding my body, beginning about 7 PM last night, continuing on going to bed about 9:30 PM, still continuing at 1:30 and 6 AM this morning. Not very pleasant. (Do NOT try to tap into this energy. It is not for others to sample yet.)

January 26, 1993. The following letter was sent to a very close friend. It is presented here to show one of the ways that unique, new individuals are presently being brought forth and developed. B— is now about 5 years old and will become one of our supreme guides in the future. For her baptism several years ago her father asked me for (and received) some of the water I had brought back from the River Jordan. (While this was not necessary for her development, it speeded up and refined her development process somewhat.) At the party following her baptism, we gave to her mother (to be held for her) a large, gold Alaskan nugget (representing the Earth), some frankincense (representing the spirit), and myrrh (representing God). The latter two of these I obtained in Jerusalem during my trip there. This couple is now divorcing. In the last year or so, I have also identified a young boy, about 5 years old, who will also become one of our guides. No letter such as this has yet been sent to his parents or grandparents. This would not be desirable for his development at this time.

Jan.25, 1993
Dear C—,
We're sorry you won't be able to make it here (for a visit) but those things happen and it's no big deal. We'll look forward to seeing the two of you when you can—later this year—or the next—or the next.

"All is going well with you now—whether you know it or not—so there is no urgency about a visit. The very fact that the divorce is going ahead was the most important item for you and at last it is underway. Don't worry about the money. All that you need is being provided to you. Continue to use what you receive with the same care you are presently using."

(Obviously **DK** has taken over here.)

"Lower your intensity of concern over men and take a more relaxed attitude. You don't have to look at each one as a possible mate. Think more of each as an interesting companion for the moment, learning about each as each is presented to you. You are much too serious about such contacts. There's no need for your evaluation of each one at this present stage. Enjoy these contacts as they expand your knowledge of mankind.

"When the time is right—not for some time yet—you

will be given the chance to consider the possibility of a new mate. But right now simply allow your energy to flow out to all others and watch and learn what happens. Consciously send it out. Your mind is not nearly complete enough (she is in her thirties) right now for any serious considerations. Yes, your mind and its capabilities are still continuing to grow and they will continue to do so for many years yet. With—(her husband) abdicating his role of guiding B—, you were chosen to take over and do what his soul had decided that he should do. Fear not. You are now being taught all those things that he was to teach her. You won't understand any of the things that I am talking about now, but that is of no consequence. As you become capable of teaching her, your thoughts and actions will begin flowing into her and she will learn without you or her realizing what is going on. But you will be startled by some of her actions as she begins to grow far beyond human capabilities.

"Continue to nourish and enrich her and her environment as you have been doing. Begin to play down her physical appearance and concentrate more on her mental capabilities—the joy of mental accomplishments. These games should be whatever you or she wish them to be. You needn't control these and you needn't be concerned about specifically what you work on. This will be like physical training to the human. Her mind needs to be exercised also! Help it along and glory in its accomplishments.

"I think this is enough startling information for you to handle right now. Treat this information as privileged information, handled in any way that you see fit.

"All our love and thoughts."

DK (and initially HK)

221

After typing this letter into this record, I remembered two other letters that I had recently sent to C— about her divorce that also have large sections by **DK** in them. Since his comments might also be helpful to others going through such a trying time I have included them here.

Oct. 24, 1992

Dear C—,

As always it was a pleasure to hear from you and find you to be in good spirits—but posing some interesting questions.

First, you wondered what you had done in a previous life to have such painful karma?

"You did nothing! You must realize that you chose this particular life—and these contacts—to further develop your soul. We are all continuing to learn and grow here and came here for this particular purpose. If there were no particular challenges and interesting situations we would learn very little. What we must not do is what your husband is doing and that is to run away and hide from our responsibilities and life's situations. After all, we chose those particular situations to learn from! We must meet them head on—as you are doing. While they are often not enjoyable (what would we learn from just joy?) they develop our ability to begin to understand what life is, why we are here, and why we have chosen this particular place in our infinite life path as the best place to learn what we need now in our development.

"Enjoy these challenges! They are developing you far beyond what you realize. Don't be sad that they are happening. Realize that they are making you into something that you were not—a more nearly complete person! You are just beginning to realize that each of us is yet incomplete and each of us is struggling to learn and grow. Know

that you are progressing much faster than many. Know that it is all worth while and worth every bit of the temporary pain and suffering that you, and all of us, are constantly exposed to. Know that each challenge brings us something new and exciting and different to learn about. Remember each but don't dwell on it. It is now the past with many more wonderful challenges to enjoy and learn from and with growth yet to come.

"Don't be concerned that you are alone. You are NOT. We are all with you constantly. All you have to do to know us is to sit or lie back in the quiet—where ever you are—then relax and send out your mental thoughts to us (i.e. to your God or The Lord or Christ or Buddha or The Messiah or Yawha or Allah or Krishna or Vishnu or Shiva or to the Spiritual Hierarchy). Then smile and be happy and feel us within you. We are always there to help you and offer you comfort and advice or suggestions. You have but to ask! You will feel and know our spiritual LOVE for you whenever you ask. It is quite different from physical love. Far less demanding and far more giving and far more capable of giving you the LOVE and comfort you want and desire. And far more understanding of the trials you have subjected yourself to. We offer you the world. You have but to ask for it. (But don't be surprised by it. It will not be what you expect!)"

(Note: All readers can do this exercise as well. However this may take some practice so don't expect instant results. On the other hand you may have results quickly. There is no way to tell for sure. It depends on the capabilities of each.)"

"Concerning —(a male friend) remember what we told you in our last letter. He is your Soul Mate. That is why you have such intense feelings for him. That does NOT mean you should become his wife or lover. But it does not mean that you should not. That is entirely up to you and him in this lifetime—and NOT your individual Souls! We will not offer you any advice on this because it is something VERY personal and something you MUST work out for yourselves. Being a Soul Mate means that in one or more past lives your soul and his were One and that an inseparable bond was formed between them. However, each new existence is unique and must be carried forth on its own, not dependent on past developments or contacts.

"Be not concerned about your husband's lack of contact with B—. It is best at this time. She is a very loving person but must learn that not everyone else is so loving and understanding. We are all different but she is unique! Such lessons will be hard for her to grasp but, painful as they are, she MUST learn them or the outside world may be too much for her delicate and exquisite soul! She is doing fine with this problem and is learning her lesson. Don't try to reduce its effectiveness or minimize it, but also there is no need to emphasize or point it out to her. Simply say that is how some people are and not everyone is as loving and caring as she is.

"You did ask why —(your husband) is so uncaring about her. He is not uncaring, just unknowing. He has never properly grown up and has not learned yet how he affects others. Most children think only of themselves and he is still in this phase. There is no way you can correct this. He must do it for himself. It may not happen in this lifetime, or he may suddenly turn around. There is no way to know since he must go through some experience that has the capability to change his realization of himself and others. He must then grasp and learn from that experience. It is unknown whether he will be able to do this.

"With all our LOVE and love"

Dec.3, 1992
My dear C—,
What a sad letter your letter of Nov. 30 was concerning
B— and your Soul Mate. You asked **DK** for help, but he can
only help you a little.

"You see, these are problems which relate to this particular life on Earth, and which you have chosen precisely
because of these problems! You want a nice, simple and
clear solution and there isn't one.

"B— wants her father to call and he refuses. No one
can tell her such a call is not important to her because it is.
No one can make him call her if he chooses not to as he is
obviously doing. Thus, you see, there is no nice solution.
Thus we come to the difficult problem of how to soften the
blow to her. Do you remember when you were a little girl?
Did you ever want something so badly that it hurt? And
then you didn't get it? This probably happened to you
many times as a child as it happened to all of us. Tell B—
about those times. Not all at once, but whenever she seems
to be in particular pain. Let her know that life sometimes
seems cruel to us but the pain caused during these times is
needed to make us stronger. To help us understand that we
are not going to get all the things we want or expect in life.
And tell her that even though her father and many others
love her, love is usually not expressed in the way that she
would like to have it expressed. It is expressed, by him, by
silence. He is afraid that talking to her will only make it
worse for her. (Actually he thinks he his hurting YOU by
this silence and, at the moment, this is more important to
him. But he does realize that he is also hurting her as well.)
Unfortunately, he is still a little child sometimes and is
thinking more of himself than of her and also, further,

simply doesn't know what to say to her. Can you simplify all of this so it is easier for her to understand?

"Many wonderful things will happen to us during this life—especially to B—, but most of the really wonderful things will not be what we wanted or expected. They will happen because they need to happen or because they teach us something that is needed for our future development or because we are here to make them happen. Seldom will what we consciously work for, or desire, take place as we foresaw or planned it. And after we have what we thought we were working for, we often (usually) find that it wasn't worth the effort, and wonder why we tried so hard for it. But we learned much in the trying! And what was wonderful may have been the learning of the process rather than the goal! This is all very complicated and hard to explain to a child—or even to an adult. But somehow you—and only you—must help B— over this difficulty. She will come thrugh it scarred, but much stronger. It is all part of the Great Plan!''

"Now as to your Soul Mate—I would like to say, 'Forget him. He isn't worth the trouble!' But he is! Not necessarily as a mate but as an intellectual (as well as physical) challenge. He will probably be the single greatest challenge during this period of your life—even greater than the challenge of B—because this has the potential for greater harm to you. You must come to grips with him—with all the harm or good he may cause you. The ultimate solution would be for you two to become fast friends and no more. But that may not be possible. Only you two can work that out and come fully to grips with this intense love/fear relationship. I would suggest that you explore this challenge very cautiously, with as much time between each contact as possible. This will give the lessons learned during each contact time to more fully sink in, and be realized and understood. Don't expect anything more than friendship to come out of it. If it does—because you believe that it must—then expect many problems that you can't foresee, to occur, but also much love. (Not the total love that you wish but perhaps enough for you.)

"So far you have been handling the problem well, but it would be so easy to let it get out of hand. That would eventually be disastrous because you must continue this relationship with greater caution than you realize. Only in this way can you work out many problems before they occur, and thus reduce the possibility of their destroying your relationship—whatever it is.

"With all our best wishes for a truly happy Christmas and a wonderful New Year."

DK (and HK)

February 6, 1993, 5:30 PM. I was suddenly lead to my collection of crystals and then guided to an Azurite crystal cluster I had purchased several years ago. I was told to hold it and keep it near for the next 24 to 48 hours.

February 7, 1993, 3:30 AM. With the day old full moon shining down on me through the glass pyramid roof, as I slept in the KIVA, I was suddenly awakened and told to take the Azurite crystal from my pajama breast pocket and put it on my forehead. As I did so I immediately began feeling a new and different kind of vibration throughout my whole body. At 4:00 AM the moon disappeared from my view and I was told that I could now get up and write this note down. My whole body is continuing to vibrate to this new energy as I go back to bed.

Feb.26, 1993, 5:30AM: Statement on Politics:

"Politics has been stated as being the art of compromise. This is true. However, when the compromise involves trading one evil for another evil or one injustice for another injustice then this is not politics but more evil (whatever that evil may be at the time.) For instance, when a politician forces other politicians to agree to a farm subsidy (provided by all citizens) on tobacco, to encourage its growth, knowing that the resultant tobacco, when smoked, will cause harm to not only the smoker but others in the area as well, then both groups of politicians are committing evil and each will be harmed—either in this life or a subsequent life—as they have harmed others.

"Another example would be in the permitting of anyone to purchase lethal weapons. The vast majority of citizens wish this practice to be severely limited. And yet, over and over, such action has been prevented from taking place because of the use of wealth and pressure applied to politicians by the few who will benefit from such action. Those applying the improper pressure as well as the politicians accepting the pressure, must answer for their actions.

"Politicians often claim that they are just looking after the needs of their constituents in taking a specific action. However, those particular constituents are usually a tiny majority of their total constituents. Typically, if their total constituents were polled over such issues, the politicians would find that they are acting against the wishes of the vast majority, and therefore, in doing such, take on the full responsibility of such action.

"Another indication of political impropriety is when a politician states during their election process the they will only run for one term and then they attempt to continue in office at the next election. There can be no excuse for such action, and great harm will befall the politician for such action.

"A politician wields great power. Accordingly, great good can result from their actions. However, when they act in their own self-interests, rather than for the wishes of the majority of their constituents (for instance in trying to be re-elected no matter what compromises in principles they must make to achieve it), then they institute great evil and must bear the full effects of their action."

CHAPTER 12

ANSWERS TO ANCIENT QUESTIONS

As **DK** and I became more at home with each other, I started to feel that perhaps I could ask him questions other than those that referred specifically and directly to my spiritual development. An unexpected opportunity to explore this area more thoroughly occurred after moving to Arizona when my wife and I began attending a local college course in Philosophy.

Suddenly I was being asked questions in this course that I had never really thought about in depth before. Furthermore, I wasn't very impressed with the answers given in the text books to some of these basic questions, many of which had been around for at least 2000 years. Not only didn't the texts have good answers to some of these questions—they couldn't even decided what the basic answers should be since there were many different answers to every question. For instance, consider the arguments for the existence of God. First there are answers based on natural theology which includes cosmological arguments and teleological arguments, each with many variations. Then there are ontological arguments and moral arguments. Then there are nonrational approaches or arguments including many kinds of mysticism. And these are only the major categories of possible answers. Most of these have sub-answers as well. In other words, philosophers still haven't agreed on answers to some of the most basic questions thought up by mankind.

Is there a solution to this problem? Does anyone other than philosophers really care if there are good or correct answers? Since there are so many books available on philosophy and religion, and new ones are continually being written, there must be a desire for such knowledge. Accordingly, I asked a number of questions about religion and philosophy to **DK,** without any idea what might happen. Since he is a member of the Spiritual Hierarchy, one would think that if anyone should be able to provide such answers he should. After all, the Spiritual Hierarchy consists of those great beings who have been selected by God to help carry out his wishes. What better place to go for answers. What follows, then, are specific answers to questions, most of which our philosophy instructor posed to me, and I in turn posed to **DK.** These questions and answers were asked and received over a period of about two months during October and November, 1990.

First, let's start with one of the most important. In the face of death, who am I, and how do I know?

"The opening part of the question, 'In the face of death' has no meaning or relationship to the remainder of the question since death of the body is simply a transition between different states of matter or being. At death, the entity simply leaves the physical body and journeys to an interdimensional place where full consciousness and awareness and growth can continue as directed by the individual soul.

"The question, 'Who am I' is much more difficult to answer because it contains many sub-questions. But, in general, each of us is a unit of energy which is eternal and which can, and has, evolved from extremely primitive

232

states. That is, from less than mineral, through mineral, to what we think of as living organisms. As a living organism we began as a simple organic molecule, then moved on to a one cell creature, then to multi-cell entities, then to plants, then to creatures with motion, and finally to our present state with what we call a thinking brain.

"At each stage—including prior to mineral—we had consciousness and the ability to think although this ability has constantly expanded as we grew and learned. Actually we currently misuse the word 'think' when we apply it to ourselves. We must differentiate and separate this thought into four components: 1) the thought, 2) the thought process, 3) the thinker, and 4) the brain. The thinker is the entity which we refer to as 'I.' The other three are just part of the process!

"The next question which typically arises is, 'If this is so, where am I going after death (of this body)?' The 'where' is too difficult to explain with our present language and knowledge, but the purpose of this, and all past and future life is to reach a point in our growth where 1) we become enlightened, 2) we begin to encompass that which we are, and 3) we truly merge with God, and yet still maintain our identity, much as a rain drop can merge with a river, and then the ocean, and yet still maintain its 'raindropness.'

"The terms 'enlightened' and 'that which we are' cannot be explained well enough to make them truly meaningful, except to state that they are stages beyond our present human-Homo sapiens state. Some advanced individuals are just now reaching the beginning of the state we call enlightened. Eventually all will enter this state and beyond. This state of enlightenment will create individuals who are greater in difference than that between Cro-

Magnon Man and Modern Homo sapiens."

In answer to the question "How do I know these things?," the answer can only be "I and my master are one," and that which he knows, I know—provided my intellect is capable of understanding his thoughts.

Now lets go to the next big question. First, "What is the difference between god and God?" Second, "Who or what is God"—assuming that there is such a being in the first place?

First, lets see how a fairly current dictionary defines them. The American Heritage Dictionary (1969) defines "god" as follows (the first definition only): "A being of supernatural powers or attributes, believed in and worshipped by a people; especially a male deity thought to control some part of nature or reality or to personify some force or activity."

It then goes on to define "God" as "A being conceived as the perfect, omnipotent, omniscient originator and ruler of the universe, the principal object of faith and worship in monotheistic religions."

Now lets correctly answer these questions.

"Actually both definitions are incorrect because they give those definitions that held for only a relatively short period of time. The word 'god' was never really in use for any prolonged period of time. It was either 'God' or nothing. The word 'god' therefore is specific to only our age and should be dropped since the beings it refers to are obsolete and have been replaced with one or more of our present Gods.

"The word 'God,' while partially correct in referring to a being who is the principal object of faith and worship in monotheistic religions, is quite incorrect in referring to this being as 'The originator and ruler of the universe.' The term 'God' should only refer to the being who governs this planet."

(HK note: this being is also often referred to as "The Ancient of Days," "The One Initiator," "The Lord of the World," "Sanat Kumara," or one of many other names in various texts).

"**The term to specify the originator and ruler of the universe should be 'GOD.'**

"**With these definitions in place we can now begin to try to answer question two which is, 'What is God?' This answer will also try to justify the answer just given to question one.**

"**If one studies human history on Earth, it becomes fairly obvious that mankind began its climb to civilization through a series of steps typically defined as the band, the tribe, the chiefdom, and the state. In EVERY CASE, in order for the unit (whatever it was) to exist, and survive, there had to be a leader, or chief, or small group, who made the decisions that had to be made to keep anarchy and then disaster from befalling the group and destroying what had already been built. Chaos is the result of lack of successful leadership or organization. The larger the number of entities involved and/or the complexity of the organization, the more important is the need for clear, precise, and decisive leadership. Where ever there is a lack of such leadership, or control, and its related effective organization, disintegration must take place—as repeatedly seen on Earth in many groups, tribes, states and civilizations of the past and present. Precise and specific rules or laws must be engendered to help with the control of organizations, whatever kind they may be.**

"**This requirement for leadership is true not only for humanity but for much of the animal and insect world that has any kind of organization as well. For instance, those animals that live and hunt in packs—such as wolves—have a clearly defined leader. Gorillas have the same thing as do** lions. In the insect world, ants and bees are prime examples of highly organized creatures. If one looks at man himself (or any multi-cell creature), the organization of the millions of differing cells within each body requires an organization of exceptional perfection. When this organization fails, sickness and death usually follow, often with unexpected swiftness. If one begins to look on the sub-cell unit—the molecule and on down to the atom—one sees again organization and rules governing them.

("Many of these rules are just now beginning to be determined).

"If one then goes the other way and looks at the planetary and cosmic scale, again we see organization and rules governing motion and life, rules and laws that have been in existence for untold billions of years, even if, today, we aren't able to determine many of these laws and rules.

"If one then looks at successful organizations, it becomes obvious that at each new order of complexity a new and efficient organization must be evolved to direct and control it if it is to live and successfully grow. On Earth we call that supreme leader God. Without such a leader, the unbelievably complex living entity we call Earth could not possibly have evolved and grown to its present degree of organization and sophistication. Likewise, the unbelievably more complex universe could not be what it is without an even greater and more perfect GOD."

Most of the questions asked here were posed by our philosophy instructor, F. Anderson. After **DK** answered his initial questions, Mr. Anderson would sometimes ask further questions which **DK** then answered. The next answer is one such addition.

"What is the source of such wisdom?" (referring to the answer just given and to other answers in this chapter).

"The answers come from whatever source is believed to be able to give the clearest and most correct answers. This can vary from God or The Christ, through the various Masters to initiates or disciples. The intelligence typically called 'Mother Earth' or 'Pacha Mama' also comes through on occasion. In general, the Master Djwhal Khul, whom HK is closest to, will answer most of the questions because he is one with him, and knows and understands the requirements and the intelligence which he has to work with."

(HK note: The provider of the information typically does not identify themselves unless specifically asked)

This is another such second question from the instructor: "If, as you claim, 'I and my Master are one,' and 'That which he knows, I know,' then why is there a need for learning? How does one improve on perfection? How does one know he/she is understanding correctly?"

"HK and I have formed an inseparable bond between us. This is not a bond in flesh but in spirit. An electrical analogy would be there is a current flowing between us which cannot be broken no matter how far apart we are. As such, I can talk to him, and he can do the same to me, at any place and at any time. We talk with our minds, not with vocal cords as you do. While we are one, we each are still separate individuals and have not yet merged our minds. This final fusion will occur when all mankind reaches the state were all can fuse with God, that is, become one with that great entity. Until then we remain as individuals but able to exchange thoughts, energies, etc.

"As to your question, 'How does one know if he/she is understanding correctly?' when one talks with the mind, there is much less of of a chance of a misunderstanding.

However, a slight misunderstanding is always possible since I must talk through his mind, with its learned meanings and cultural implications. However, we are so close that, if there is a question of meaning between us, we both realize it, and I will sometimes offer a substitute word, or I will look into the mind of the person reading the words and request that he use the word I originally suggested."

Now lets get to the third philosophical "biggie." "Is there such a thing as free will for mankind, or are we just actors on a stage?" Let's put this chestnut to bed once and for all!

"**Mankind exists to express free will! The reason the Earth is populated with human souls is to allow each individual intelligence to grow in understanding and capability. Without free will there could be no growth in understanding and accordingly no reason to incarnate.**

"**Each individual requiring further development consciously selects their individual time period, and then their desired culture, and then finally selects their specific parents, so they can be given the desired environment in which to grow and be able to attack the one or more problems which they themselves feel it is necessary for them to be able to understand and solve before they can grow further in ability and spirituality.**

"**Many times they will not be successful in learning what they, themselves, believe they need to learn, and will have to come back again—and again?—before THEY feel they have mastered the lesson(s) which they feel they must learn for their further development.**

"**With this understanding of the use of the Earth for such lessons, it becomes obvious that free will is essential for the possibility for growth. If there were no free will, there could be no possibility for learning—either through success or failure—and accordingly there would be no rea-**

son to incarnate in the first place.

"Further, what would be the purpose of birth at all if there was no free will? As a toy for God? This is obviously absurd. God has created the Earth to help developing souls to grow as God is continuing to grow (No, God is not perfect yet either. Growth continues for all).

"As mankind, individually and collectively, grows, they reach specific stages where they can go on to other areas of the universe for further instructions and lessons—which they themselves continue to select since the individual Soul knows what is required for its further growth—something which it feels in its desire to become ONE, first with God, and finally GOD."

This most interesting answer brings up another question, however. If this is true, how does the soul know what is required for its growth?

"The Soul knows the Great Plan of God for it and all other Souls. This was impressed on it during its creation. It can then match what the entity has learned with what remains to be done, giving the lower self enough information to permit it to make its own decisions—in conjunction with input from the Soul, but without burdening the lower self with so much information that it becomes confused or gives up at the enormity of the task and the distance yet to be travelled."

In addition to the above question and answer, the previous answer also brought up two other questions. The first of these is: "You state that one's incarnation is the consequences of an act of will. That each individual consciously selects his/her culture, even parents. This is a wholly counter-evidential claim. How do you defend/support this view? What possible evidence is there for it?"

"How could one prove this statement? What evidence

do you require? We are simply stating facts here. If you understand the laws of the conservation of energy, then you would understand that all the energy expended in living a life on Earth—and learning all that is learned—would not be wasted on death, but would be retained for future use and growth. You must understand that there is no point in simply living one life on Earth. From the time life—of any kind—was capable of living on Earth, cells of life were brought here (from other star systems) to learn and grow. As each cell died, the inorganic and organic matter returned to the Earth and the Life Energy then, sooner or later, returned to Earth to continue its growth. This has been happening for eons of time, the Life Energy eventually reaching its highest present state of development on Earth in these entities you call mankind. Growth continues for mankind and will continue for perhaps many eons further depending on the speed that mankind grows to the point where God considers that you can grow no further in this environment. Then you, that is, mankind, or at least those entities who have developed sufficiently will go to other solar systems, in this or other galaxies, where growth can continue. It is a wonderful development to look forward to, is it not?

"In the meantime those of you who have developed far enough so far—and almost everyone is at a different stage of development—are just now being readied for a jump into the next stage of capability on Earth. It is a stage which roughly corresponds to the difference between Cro-Magnon Man and Modern man, although the jump this time will be considerably greater than this last step. The first individuals with this vastly expanded capability will begin appearing before the year 2000, and will not initially be babies, but will be fully developed individuals. Their bodies are currently being changed by us much as a butterfly changes physically in going from a caterpillar to the butterfly."

The third question brought up by the answer about God is "What is the source for making the distinction between god and GOD (and God)?"

"The source was God, as described to DK, then through the mind and fingers of the entity you know as H.King. The process for the transfer of wisdom such as this cannot be described to you in greater detail because you don't have the understanding of the energies which are involved in such a transfer. It will be centuries before mankind even begins to have the mental capacity for such understanding and it will be millennia before a true knowledge of the process is available."

Now comes another interesting question and, perhaps, one basic to this whole book: "What method or methods, criterion or criteria enable you to discern between wisdom/truth on the one hand and illusion/falsehood on the other?"

"This is a difficult question to answer because wisdom and truth are not always the same. The same holds true for illusion and falsehood. Even the single word wisdom is very difficult to define or even describe as is illusion. Furthermore even truth and falsehood can be sometimes difficult to distinguish between. However, no methods or criteria are used here. Rather, thousands of years of experience and observations tends to give one a better understanding of the human psyche, and the processes that are used within the human intelligence to reach conclusions that might be considered by it to be true or false, wisdom or illusion. I (DK) know of no satisfactory method or criteria for determining such."

All these answers, while fascinating, bring up another basic question as follows: "If each individual has the kind of autonomy and power indicated, what role is there for God or GOD?"

"**God is primarily concerned with the growth of mankind as a whole—with the growth of the Soul which is the final development of the Life Cells or Life Units on Earth. God and the assistants selected for this task (such as The Christ and The Buddha and further down the chain I (DK) and several others) work through mankind, placing situations and thoughts before, and through, certain individuals, to permit further growth and understanding. (These individuals, of course, are free to accept and utilize or ignore these thoughts or make wrong decisions about the situations placed before them. This is all part of the learning process.) These notes to you are part of this learning experience.**

"**GOD, while concerned about each individual cell in the universe, is concerned primarily with the growth of entire star systems and galaxies. Each of these has a life of its own just as mankind has a life of his or her own. Think of each of the cells in your body as a star system, each independent but interacting with other cells and groups of cells. Then you can realize how GOD is concerned with the whole body just as God is concerned with your present body as it interacts with other bodies and groups of bodies.**"

Now let's go back to the question on free will. The philosophy instructor wasn't convinced by this answer—perhaps because he had never heard anything quite like it—and wanted more information. His question was as follows: "Given what you state about free will, it is obviously possible to be wrong.

"How do you know that you are right? If there is no clear arbiter against which I can access the rightness or correctness of my assertions then such distinctions as 'right,' 'wrong,' and 'true' and 'false' lose any meaning. One is left with a purely subjectivistic egoistic perspective: 'This is true because I believe it is true.' How do you break out of this subjectivism?"

"How do you know that any philosopher is right? They give proof which isn't proof at all. It is simply a collection of facts and ideas which you either agree with or reject. Yet you go to a scientists who has collected proof and facts and accept these, even though they are based on half truths, or simple observations—sometimes repeated by others and sometimes not.

"There are very few things that can be considered absolute in this world—and even most of these will be challenged in the next few hundred years. Thus you are left with ideas which seem to have validity to you and which you enjoy arguing with. Consider my ideas as such, since there is no other way I can get you to even consider them. Show them to your peers and see if you can come up with more specific questions which I can try to answer for you."

This answer very graphically points out the major problem in working in this field. Since it is not based on a material that you can measure and weigh and otherwise specify, how can you prove anything? As you can see, questions often aren't specific enough to obtain the answers that convince you. And, without convincing answers, better questions are difficult to come up with. What it boils down to is that philosophers should now concentrate on coming up with better and more specific questions rather than trying to guess at answers that aren't even close to reality.

Now lets go to another basic question of the philosopher: "Select an example of "evil" and explain it." Philosophers love to talk about "evil" because they think there is so much of it around, and it is something that everyone has an opinion on. I think you will be surprised at **DK**'s answer!

"**The dictionary previously cited defines 'evil' as 'Morally bad or wrong, wicked, malevolent; sinful.' These are all local, cultural terms of a specific time period and have no absolute meaning. It can only be partially described when a particular locality and precise time period is defined, and because this is constantly changing, a discussion of it is essentially meaningless.**"

The instructor didn't think much of this answer so he tried again with a variation of this basic question. This time, I think he got an answer which surprised him in a totally different way than the previous answer, but it clarifies so much! His question was: "From what you wrote, "evil" is a meaningless concept. What about suffering? And what about "unfair suffering"?

"**Suffering is due to what you think of as evil and is ALWAYS due to the entity involved having performed some act which it knows was wrong at the time of performing the act or acts.**

"**The entity must learn that such an act is wrong and must not be repeated. In order to be sure that the entity has learned its lesson, what you call suffering is inflicted on the individual by its higher self, or Soul, either in the life when the act occurs, or in one or more subsequent lives. (Reincarnation is a fact whether you choose to believe it or not!) If the test as to whether the entity has learned its lesson is to occur in a subsequent life, the Soul will typically select a particular life and situation where a condition will exist, which exposes the entity to the situation which will prove whether the individual has learned their lesson or not. In any case, there must be a punishment for committing the act in the first place. This is the suffering that you ask about.**

"**The Christian religion (and many others as well) talk**

about going before God at death to have one's deeds weighed. This is not correct. Each individual (that is, its lower self), meets with it's own Soul on death, to determine what lessons have been learned, and what situations are necessary in the next life to grow, learn and correct past errors."

(HK note: Some time ago I was asked if I could help heal the sister of an acquaintance of mine. This sister suffers from epilepsy. I asked **DK** about it and he said that I must not interfere. She had chosen this disease, in this life, to expiate past errors, and if I cured her, she would have to repeat the problem in a subsequent life. However, it was perfectly OK for her sister to get regular medical help, since this does not tap into psychic energy).

Another favorite question of the philosopher is whether we have souls. We have talked about this enough in this book so far, that I'm sure that by now you are aware of what **DK**'s answer to this will be. However, in this section he fleshes out his answer somewhat, so you can understand it a little better. Question: "Do humans have souls?"

"There can be no direct proof of the Soul to someone else—only to the individual who is interested in determining the fact for themselves. For this individual, the proof occurs when direct contact with the Soul is made, and subsequent communication occurs. For each individual this first contact will be different, depending on the individual's past history including such things as religion, beliefs (typically quite different, even for members of the same family), reason for contact, age, sex, country of origin and present location, and such things as individual study or knowledge from human contact.

"Soul contact occurs when the Soul decides contact is necessary to achieve some specific purpose. It is not con-

sciously or knowingly initiated by the individual. In general, the Soul will not advise the individual what the contact is for, but will simply make a statement on which the individual is supposed to ponder and learn from. Contact will be made in such a way that the receiver will know that it has occurred and that it did not happen in a dream."

(HK note: I have already discussed my Soul contact during my trip to Kashmir, India, and **DK**'s subsequent comments about it).

Now comes the next obvious question "How do you know that 'soul-contact' isn't merely an hallucination? How does one know that he/she isn't dreaming?" This is another question that is really key to almost this entire book. How do you know that this whole book—and, for that matter, **DK** as well—isn't just a bunch of baloney, and one continuous hallucination?

"It is fairly easy to tell whether you are dreaming or not, if one defines dreams as occurring during a state of sleep. When you are talking to someone else, and they can verify and repeat what you said sometime later, or when you can type something down—as we are doing now—and the record remains—then you are fairly sure that one is not dreaming.

"To prove that it is not an hallucination is much more difficult—especially to someone else. If we define 'Hallucination' as something that you believe you heard or saw, but no one else present heard or saw it, then it is easy to call the mental transmission of thoughts a hallucination. However, if the receiver of thoughts repeats these thoughts as they are received, and these thoughts contain information that sounds or feels true, or acceptable, and the hearer is fairly sure that the speaker doesn't know this information, then the hearer isn't quite so sure that there is a hallucination involved.

"Actually the best way to come to grips with this problem is for the hearer to learn to channel themselves. And it is important that this attempt be made in all seriousness, and with some effort. If this is not done, the criticiser then simply becomes someone who is either afraid to prove to themselves that this might be possible, or has a closed mind and refuses to even believe that such a thing is possible, and is therefore not honest with themselves or their audience.

"Learning to channel is not nearly as difficult as it sounds, although it requires the hearer to 1) believe that such a transmission is possible (obviously if you don't believe it is possible then you won't accept anything that happens), 2) is willing to talk to their ego and mentally, temporarily, set it aside so it can't interfere with the transmission"

An ancient Tibetan technique for this is to take the ego and put it into a mentally created pitcher, then pour the contents of the pitcher into a nearby lake or stream which you have also mentally created. Be aware, however, that after you have done that the first time or two, you may have a great feeling of emptiness within you for a short time. Don't fear that the ego won't return! It will often return before you wish it to, and when you finally realize that it is back, you will have to tell it to go away again!

Actually, after using this technique successfully several times, my ego suddenly told me that it didn't much care for this process of being put into a pitcher, and then poured into a stream. What a surprise that was to suddenly be talking to the ego—and having an intelligent conversation with it as well!! So we worked out a compromise! Instead of being shoved into a pitcher, we simply (mentally) walked together into a beautiful, warm greenhouse that I also mentally created, that was full of beautiful plants and birds, and I then walked back out through the door, closing it behind me and leaving the ego in a place it enjoyed very much. You (and your ego) may have other ideas about places for it to temporarily go. In any case, the ego may still come out before you are ready. You'll know this when you suddenly realize that you are having thoughts that are self-centered instead of globally centered. When you realize this, then simply mentally take the ego back to its resting place for another rest, and continue your channeling.

"The third step to begin channeling is for the hearer to be aware that the first time or two that you invite your Master to enter your mind, you may feel a great fear that you will be taken over, welling up within you. When this occurs, the beginning of the transmission immediately stops, and you will have to go through the procedure again, sometime in the future, for this is an entirely voluntary procedure which you can always stop if you wish."

This happened to me and for a while I didn't know how to deal with it. However, I quickly found that I simply had to try it again.

"Remember, your Master ONLY comes in when invited. Also remember that you absolutely have 'free will' which can NEVER be taken away from you!

"People often think that an evil spirit will come in in this way. The chances of this occurring are infinitesimally small. However, you would immediately know if such a thing occurred, because you would feel the energy—not through fear, but through its evilness—and you could then easily and immediately break off the transmission just by wishing it!

"Once you have developed contact with your Master then you will 1) know that you are not dreaming, and 2) be relatively sure that it is not an hallucination. However, this second step will take considerably longer because prior

beliefs and training are very hard to erase.

"Sometime after you have established a dialog with your Master (This will probably take several tries before you have sufficiently strengthened the bond or contact to receive a strong and clear transmission), your Soul or Higher Self may come in. Others may then follow, if they feel that they have something to contribute.

"The ability to heal yourself and others often then follows if you wish—and your physical structure is capable of transmitting the necessary energies—although this capability usually takes considerable time to develop. Your Master will usually tell you if your present body is capable of this, without you asking. But don't expect such information right away. This may take many months or years before you know for sure, and then it may take additional time before the capability has flowered within you."

(HK note: One thing that has been very carefully and thoroughly drilled into me is the absolute necessity of patience in any such undertaking. While I am a slow learner, and it may have taken me much longer than you to reach any particular stage, you must not expect instantaneous results. The Masters want those who are committed and willing to work for results—not those following a temporary whim! The energies that you will be dealing with can be dangerous to wield—for the wielder as well as the subject—so you must understand what you are dealing with, and that can't happen overnight.)

In closing this chapter, let's ask a fairly recent question that has more and more meaning in many fields as our awareness increases. "Do trees have rights?"

"In order to discuss this subject, the word 'rights' must be specified. Are these rights the right to exist? The right to grow unhindered? The right to not be cut down? The right to grow to maturity and die of old age as humans do? The right to expand into new areas or the right to maintain existing areas? And, if so, does this mean new plantings in that area if there are cuttings, or must the current plants be left alone?

"Each of these questions deserves its own argument depending on whether one is talking about the tree as an individual entity, or is concerned about the loss of the oxygen it produces, or the beauty of it—either alone, or in a grove, or in a forest. Very complicated!

"To try to simplify the problem, let us try to see what a tree is—or perhaps what it is not. First, trees have consciousness, as everything on this planet has consciousness—including rocks and the Earth itself (Mother Earth or Pacha Mama)! However, the consciousness of rocks and trees—excluding Mother Earth—is not yet like that of humans, in that they have not individualized yet. Rather, their consciousness is a group consciousness, and the members of a particular group changes as the question addressed to them changes. This would be much like the fact that someone representing the United States would probably answer a question referring to it as an entity, differently than if a similar question were asked of a state or a local government, because of the different viewpoints and requirements that would be considered.

"Realizing that all things on Earth—including the Earth itself—have a consciousness—whether individualized or collective—we then can go back to the original question, 'Do trees have rights?' The answer, must, of course, be that they do, since we do not have the right to give or take away such rights in the first place. Only God has that right!

"Now, however, if we then further ask the question, 'Do we as humans have the right to selectively remove and utilize some of the products of the Earth?,' the answer is yes, PROVIDED that we remove and utilize such products judiciously. We do NOT have the right to so remove some product, that its continued existence and ability to reproduce (or entities which depend on it for their existence and ability to reproduce), is hindered in any way! We do NOT have the right to waste any resource, whatever it may be. We do NOT have the right to destroy significant areas of the Earth through removal, addition, or change!

"Centuries and millennia ago we had neither the technology nor desire to change large areas of the Earth's surface. With the acquisition of the capability, and the desire, to do so, it has now become necessary for us to more fully utilize our rapidly evolving consciousness—both individual and collective. (Note that we as humans—with our recently greatly expanded ability to communicate—are finally developing a collective consciousness, something the mineral and plant kingdom have had for millennia.) We must control the greed of those among us who have proved their inability to identify and control it in themselves. The term greed must also be used to define those among us who insist or demand that they be able to produce as many children as they wish. The Earth can no longer support the expanding population which it now has. The human population must not only stop expanding, but must actually begin to shrink, if new disasters are not to strike."

One question raised by this last answer is—"What is consciousness? How do you know that trees have consciousness? How do you know that you aren't being deceived?"

"Consciousness is the ability to recognize differences in the environment. Typically it is also associated with the ability to communicate, although this is not necessarily so. Communication can be with other parts of the same being, or with other members of the same species, or with other species. Humans use the word 'telepathic' to indicate the transmission of thoughts or ideas between individuals. However, much greater abilities than this are possible once the brain cells are adjusted to pick up and transmit thoughts of other lifeforms. Once this adjustment has occurred (I made this adjustment to HK about two years ago of your time), and the brain begins to accept the fact that other thoughts are surrounding the individual, he/she finally begins to accept the possibility of their existence, and can then first listen in, and finally communicate with the transmitter of those thought forms. It is a startling occurrence for humans when this first occurs—especially when you begin detecting thoughts from trees and rocks!

"How to prove this? How to know that it is not delusion? There is no answer to this. When it occurs, you know that it is happening. But you question even yourself. Perhaps this is the best proof to yourself—that you question it. There is no way yet possible to help someone else tune into your thoughts, so they can listen to the conversation. The best that can be done is to simply repeat the conversation out loud. If it is an intelligent conversation then the listener begins to wonder—especially if it contains information that neither the speaker nor listener is aware of. Beyond that there is great difficulty.

"HK first had a series of interchanges with trees when he was hiking in the redwoods of Big Sur in California in 1989. He first felt a great sadness about him, and then the trees began to tell him of the fact that, with the inception of the chain saw, the redwood trees were being cut down faster than they could grow, and their time on Earth was limited, unless mankind learned to control himself and his insatiable quest for profit. As he questioned them, he found

that they spoke from a collective consciousness, not from individual trees. But how to prove it? Shortly after that, at his home site in Arizona, he was questioned by a visitor as to whether they could remove a few rocks. He asked the rocks how they felt about it? Their statement (that it didn't really matter because their time on Earth as beings was so much longer than that of human entities, or even the race of man, that a move to another location is really of little consequence), so startled him that he didn't require much other proof that there was communication. But how to prove it to others? I fear there is no way."

(HK note: Many years ago my wife and I were fascinated by trees grown in very small pots, called Bonsai, by the Japanese who apparently developed the process. We purchased books on them and grew several of our own. While living in New Hampshire we also joined a nearby Bonsai growers association. After we had been a member for about a year (about 1989), and while we were attending one of their meetings where many Bonsai plants were on display and were being pruned and shaped, I suddenly began to feel a great unhappiness about me. I tried to locate this unhappiness and found it coming from the plants. I mentally questioned them and they said the following:

"We are very unhappy plants because we are never allowed to reach our magnitude. We send out new shoots so that we can grow larger and they are cut off. We send out new roots to support our new growth that we are trying to achieve and they are trimmed off. We are continually starved for food, just being given enough to survive, not flourish.

"We may be beautiful and artistic to humans who own and work with us, but we are not being permitted to grow spiritually by reaching our full capability and magnitude,

CHAPTER 13

ANSWERS TO MODERN QUESTIONS

What is the deeper meaning of these revelations? And what do they prove? They don't prove anything in scientific terms—but some very interesting and curious statements have come through the explorative mind of the author, that may require further consideration. Could they be true and correct even if, perhaps, they aren't believable? Is it possible that Christ or God or Pacha Mama or a **DK** could speak through someone? Is it possible that someone can grow spiritually?

Both the Old and New Testaments discuss The Christ Energy (The Lord or the Messiah) returning to Earth in the future. But these books don't discusses in what FORM this might occur. Part of the Hindu scriptures, The Bhagavad-Gita ("The Song of God") describes this possibility clearly and directly when Sri Krishna says "When goodness grows weak, when evil increases, I make myself a body. In every age I come back to deliver the holy, to destroy the sin of the sinner, to establish righteousness." (from The Song of God, Bhagavad-Gita, Prabhavananda & Isherwood, Mentor, 1972).

Assuming we agree that a representative of God might return to Earth, when might this occur? After the New Testament, people thought the second coming would occur within the lifetimes of the writers. In almost every age since then there

255

have been predictions that this phenomenon would occur on a particular date or year. If now, why now? **DK** says:

"Because now the time has come!"

Not very convincing if he is not a part of you, but it's the best I can do for now.

We usually assume that if someone is to come back, only one such great individual will return. But there are currently more than five billion people on Earth. During the period from about 1500 BC to about 600 AD, when most of the last group of religious founders lived on Earth, the population of the Earth has been estimated to be approximately 300 million (actually it was much less than this according to **DK**!). Furthermore, each "savior" only traveled in a very small portion of the Earth. With our now much larger population, and if we assume the same ratio of saviors to people on Earth, there would have to be twenty or thirty saviors around the world! How would we react to many saviors (perhaps even dozens) wandering the Earth, each giving their own unique message?

DK says we need to address these questions now, so that when there are multiple saviors, there won't be too much confusion and surprise, and it won't take hundreds of years to create the desired results. **DK** further says:

"You won't have that much time to waste. Time will be too critical."

In the Introduction it was stated that a new and more advanced race will be springing up amongst us very shortly. How are we going to handle this? Since this race will be both mentally and physically superior, can we expect them to simply integrate harmoniously with us or will problems occur? Should we try to segregate them and prevent them from competing with an "inferior race," or should we allow them to become our leaders because of their superior abilities? Wonderful questions to think about and debate, but we must do more than that because time will be crucial.

Let's also address the problem of major Earth changes. Will we know how to handle and be prepared for for them? In the past, all civilization was essentially destroyed. Can we do better this time? **DK** says:

"Yes, if we try hard!"

Perhaps you're now asking yourself, "If these beings that you are communicating with are so smart, why don't they give us ANSWERS to these problems?" I asked the same question, and strange or impossible to believe as it may seem, the following questions were answered either by God, the Christ, or through my Mind Bridge with **DK**. I am not sure who answered which questions, but it is of little importance, since there is a spiritual link between all, as I now have with **DK**. They are all one, as **DK** and I have become one.

October 6, 1991.

Question: Should we continue to use the present Judaic ten commandments?

" There are just three commandments for the coming new age:

"1) Do not harm others—either mentally of physically. This includes all lifeforms, not just humans. For each harm there will be greater harm to you.

"2) Work (and work honestly) for what you earn.

"3) Walk gently on this Earth of yours."

Question: What is God?

"God is that for which we wish to attain.

"God is Light and Love and Power and Energy and Life and Understanding and Will and Knowledge and Wisdom.

"God is Being

"We are all God when we wish hard enough and try hard enough."

Question: What are we here for?

"To become one with God."

Question: How do we become one with God?

"By seeking, and discovering, and following our own individual path."

Question: What is Love?

"Love is the will to help others."

Question: What is Light?

"Light is the power to help others."

Question: How should we recognize The Christ?

"By seeking The Christ within each of us. When we find this great and wonderful entity within ourselves then we will know who 'he' is without further questioning."

Question: Should God be worshipped?

"When we wish to show him our appreciation for what we have been given."

Question: How should God be worshipped?

"With our thoughts. No building, or place, or guide is necessary to teach or help us to do this."

Question: How should we visualize God?

"As a being of Wonder and Light and Love and Help."

Question: What is Nature?

"Nature is that which we are and where we are. That which surrounds us. That where we wish to be. The more we appreciate, and help, and become one with Nature, the more we are Nature, and the more Nature is us."

Question: How do we define God? That is, if not "He" or "She," then "It?"

"No. Lack of male or female does not imply no sex. Rather than no sex, imagine both male and female in one, but with a complete blending of the two. The need for the two is only for reproduction. If there is no need for reproduction, then the two similar but different characteristics

can be combined in one with the best characteristics of each, blending and fusing into one unit far superior to either. Then there is no need for the constant struggle for supremacy and uniqueness."

(HK note: Perhaps we should refer to such a being and/or ourselves when we don't wish to specify a sex as s/he or s-he or perhaps even shorter "ne"—using a letter in the alphabet about half way between h and s)

Question: Please define and explain "The Trinity," that is, The Father, The Son, and The Holy Ghost or Holy Spirit of Christianity.

"The term is really obsolete now. It attempted to explain something which is no longer necessary. Please ignore this relationship in the future."

Question: Should baptism continue to be practiced and if so, how?

"Baptism should be considered only as an acceptance of the authority of God by the one being baptized. Accordingly it should only be practiced on mature, consenting adults, never on children or babies. It should be practiced only by someone believed to be in tune with God and not by someone who has decided by himself or herself that they are such. When the individual knows that their vibrations flow between themselves and God, then they will be suitable for conducting such a ceremony.

"The ceremony itself can be conducted anywhere and at any time. The procedure is first, the placing of the palms of the hand of the transmitter onto the forehead of the individual being baptized and saying: 'With this touch I bring to you the clear white light of God and the pure golden light of Love to begin your process of enlightenment and your process of development into that of a star being.' The tips of the fingers of the transmitter may then be touched with 'The Water of God' and their life giving energies then lightly smoothed over the forehead of the individual being baptized.

"The Water of God will have been obtained by taking water from a nearby stream (never from a tap or other container) and, placing it in a simple jar or glass, will have been held against the forehead of the transmitter for a period of at least one minute, and preferably five or so minutes, while the transmitter is consciously linking him or herself with God and allowing God's vibration to descend down through the crown chakra and out through their forehead and into the water container. The Water of God should be used up within a twelve hour period and only for baptism. Any remaining fluid should be drunk by the transmitter only since its energies would be too powerful for any but very highly spiritually developed individuals."

Question: If everyone becomes a channel—and therefore a prophet—and soon begins transmitting many prophecies through many cultures and intelligences, won't it make a big mess?

"Yes. On the other hand, they will all be similar enough for their own culture that within a relatively short period of time a consensus will be arrived at, in which each culture decides for itself that that is what they want for that particular time period."

Question: This implies that one religion should no longer go out and try to convert others—especially other cultures—to their religion. Is this correct?

"Yes. Each culture should develop its own religion for itself, and no attempt should be made to interfere with it. Soon enough all will see that all the new religions are saying the same thing in different ways, and there will be just one great religion with individual variations which are desired for that time period."

Question: Is there any particular way that the dead should be buried?

"No, it makes no difference what-so-ever as to location or method of burial. Cremation is the cleanest and neatest and takes the least space, but because there is no life energy left in the body, its method of disposal is of little importance."

October 7, 1991, 2 PM

Question: In the transmission of September 28, 1991 you stated "You are being attacked by the gathered forces of evil." What evil does this refer to?

"This refers to the energies which are everywhere and which often oppose the energies which we are directing on Earth. These energies are those of past and present entities which are part of this Earth and which are continually working against what we are trying to do, and which are working for their own individual good, and against the common good for all. We often are in conflict with them and do all we can to subvert their desires and intentions. We succeed most of the time, but occasionally they, by surprise or long planning, manage to get around us before we are aware of their intentions, or in this case, before we can summon enough energy to thwart them. We may then require the help of the entity being attacked by them.

"This attack on you was the most unified and powerful attack we have ever seen and it required all our energies and all of your energies to prevent it from succeeding. From this you can see how much of a threat they consider your development and completion—which is now very soon.

"Their threat is more typically to obtain the assistance of individuals on Earth who have, or want, something they

wish to control. They are seldom as unified as this, but they fully understand you and the threat you pose to their existence and future."

October 8, 1991, 2 PM

Question: You said in our first discussion together on September 16, 1988 among many other things that "If you consider that time is an illusion it hardly matters." What do you mean by "Time is an illusion?"

"Time is like a river. It always flows downhill and you can't get it to flow uphill unless you pump it back up with energy. Well, by applying energy you can not only make it flow backwards, that is 'up hill,' but also speed it up going downhill by steepening the slope or pumping it downhill. The problem has always been how do you apply such energy and what kind of energy do you use? In any case, because time can thus be changed, unchangeable time as you think of it, is truly an illusion. It becomes like any other dimension which can be adjusted to specific requirements or desires, once you are aware of this capability and the process necessary."

Question: In our first contact on September 16, 1988, you asked me if I would like to write a book substantiating formlessness. I agreed and hoped that this book would do that. But as I read it now, I don't believe that I have substantiated it well enough. Can you give me more information that might help it to be more understandable?

"Formlessness is simply a lack of being. Energy has no form. Light has no form. Thoughts have no form. Sound has no form. Each of these simply fills—or partially fills—any container that it is put in. Thus when you receive information in this way (that is, as we are doing by my transmitting thoughts and you receiving them), the thoughts are formless and can be stored or retransmitted any way that you wish. For instance, a thought can be written onto a piece of paper as we are doing right now and it now has form which can be seen and remembered (becoming formless again) by many others. Accordingly, one should not necessarily be concerned about receiving formless information and consider it to be unreliable. Thoughts (formless) are mostly transmitted by sound (that is by speaking) (also formless) and we don't consider such sound waves as being unreliable—even if we do often misinterpret their meanings. Ideas transmitted from mind to mind have much less chance of being misinterpreted.

"If we agree that sound and thought can be formless (and intelligent), why, then, can't some beings which can be made up of light and/or energy also be formless and intelligent and not necessarily visible to our current detection apparatus (that is, our eyes)?"

October 9, 1991, 2 PM

Question: In our conversation of September 28, 1989 you stated that I was "from a different, far away galaxy" If this is true I must have traveled here at a speed far exceeding that of light—something our current technology says is impossible. Please explain.

"Your technology is wrong. Speeds of travel far exceeding those of light are easily achieved using the thought process for transport. Thus material things are not easily transported at this speed but the essence of an individual is easily transported at speeds so rapid that their speed is not usually calculated. Rather, we think of the speed as taking so long rather than by distances. For instance, your actual travel time took approximately three weeks of Earth time rather than the thousands of years it would have taken if you had traveled just at the speed of light. However, we are not transporting your body physically, only your Soul which is all we needed to obtain your essence and to then be able to build you into the many physical forms which then followed as you progressed through Earth's various time periods, up until this present time period. Thus, you see, your present physical laws are far too confining and restrictive when it comes to doing things which we may find necessary for the development of the Earth."

Question: Concerning the above answer, can you tell me in what time period my essence was brought here?

"So long ago that you can't really know it. It occurred long before those creatures that you call dinosaurs roamed the Earth and long before even animals were prevalent in any quantity, or in many forms. You were among the first of the beings to go beyond plants and to really become individualized. It has taken us that long in planning your coming forth. Now you can begin to understand why your mental and spiritual development is so important to the development of the entire Earth system, and why we have spent so much time and energy on you in the last few years. This is all that can be said about you at this time."

Question: Is psychic healing possible for others?

"1)Psychic healing is possible when the healer understands the energies that are required to perform such miracles. Not everyone is equipped to know and work with such energies. Therefore not everyone who wishes to, or thinks they can heal, can do so. However, many who are not aware of their abilities can be excellent healers if they are willing to learn how to develop these abilities.

"2) Those who have these abilities are born with it. If this ability is not inherent in you, no training can make it possible.

"3) The person with the capability and the training must understand that, even though they have the capability and training, psychic healing is not possible if the person to be healed does not wish to be healed or is not willing to make the effort necessary to bring it about. Remember, all of mankind has the right of self-determination and this can never be taken away or displaced by someone else, no matter how spiritually advanced they may be. Thus the person to be healed must not only be cooperative, but must actively take part in the healing—even though they may not understand specifically what they are doing or how they are doing it.

"4) To obtain psychic healing the healer must know the sick one. That is, they must have physically seen or touched them at one time or another (unless they are a very advanced healer) and must be able to mentally picture them in their mind as they send out healing energies. They should also know fairly specifically what the disease is that they are trying to heal and its approximate location.

"5) They must then send forth the energies which they have assembled to heal the specific disease or problem and mentally picture it arriving at the crown chakra of the person to be healed.

"6) They will then visualize that energy proceeding down from the crown chakra through the spinal column to the area requiring healing, and see that energy concentrating in that area. They will mentally keep that energy in the affected area and mentally see the disease or problem diminish and finally vanish. After a short time—perhaps one to two minutes or more—they will then allow that energy to spread throughout the body, dissipating and helping heal the remainder of the body.

"7) Depending on the psychic strength of the healer and their developed mental ability to visualize, create, and transfer energy, one or more sessions will be required to affect the healing.

"8) As previously noted in the section concerning HK's attempt to heal his brother, no chemicals or other additions of any kind should be used in conjunction with psychic healing.

"9) Remember that the patient must be fully cognizant of the attempt to heal and further, should be told when the energy has arrived at the crown chakra so they can visualize it themselves and they can then further visualize it as it moves down to the affected area. They must also see it in the affected area and further see (that is mentally picture) the problem gradually disappear.

"10) In general, problems not healed in one session should not be further treated more often than about every ten days, and two weeks would be better, so the energy does not become too concentrated in the area, and the body can take its own time in performing the final healing, clean up and recuperation.

"11) The complete process of healing often takes many weeks. So while instantaneous cures may occur, it is better to assume that they will take some time to be completed and not stress the area being repaired too rapidly.

"12) When doing psychic healing, the question is always asked as to whether traditional medicine and techniques would not be better and surer, and the time wasted in psychically attempting to heal may actually delay the final cure. The only one who can answer this question is the patient. If they strongly believe in traditional medicine, then psychic healing is truly a waste of time because it cannot work. It will work only if 1) the patient is absolutely sure that it can work and 2) if the healer is truly a psychic healer with many healings to their credit. It is interesting to note that women often have the ability to visualize energy flow more completely than men and therefore IF THEY HAVE THE ABILITY they will often make better healers."

Question: Concerning the development of individuals "on the path" (to higher understanding of spiritual laws and abilities), there is an ancient Indian saying which says "When the pupil is ready, the Master will appear." Do you have anything to add to this which may help students find and tread the path?

"This statement still holds true. The student must still wander about, trying to find what they need to progress. No Earthly teacher can help during this search. They must search all by themselves. There is no fixed time period for this initial search. It may take hours, or many lifetimes. However, once they have discovered for themselves what they are searching for—and only their Soul will know this—then help will arrive in one of many forms to assist them further in their continuing struggle to reach the Light. All are encouraged to begin this search now. They are needed desperately."

A series of statements about several subjects then came through. These statements are given next:

Statement on Cooperation vs Competition:

"Nearly all current sports and games are based on one or more individuals competing with one or more other individuals to try to prove that one—or several—are better than their competitor(s). Such sports send the message and then train the individuals—both those competing and those watching—for individual accomplishment and for individual goals.

"It would be much more desirable to develop games which show how individuals can cooperate together to achieve some particular goal, instead of trying to prove that one or more are better than others, since we are all different with our different strengths and weaknesses. If we are to succeed in building a stronger, better, and more perfect nation (whatever nation it may be) and world in our life times, we must do it through cooperation, not competition. With each individual thinking of the whole, not the one (whether person, company, city, or state) progress will be much greater and all will benefit.

"Training for such accomplishments must begin in childhood, not after graduation. Accordingly, non-competitive games would be of much value in developing such abilities and mindset."

Statement on Wealth vs Helping Others:

"Nearly all nations tend to glorify individuals and companies for making the most money. Some magazines even print lists of those individuals who have accumulated the most wealth, or those companies which have been the most profitable in the last year. This is disgusting, and a measure of how far a society can go wrong. Instead we should be glorifying those individuals and companies who have helped others the most—those who have most successfully utilized their funds and knowledge for helping individuals or groups or towns or states the most!

"We must remember that all wealth flows from God. The thing to remember is not how much we have earned or accumulated but how much good we have done with what we have been given. How much better to discuss those who are most efficient or creative in using their wealth—however much it may be, even the tiniest amount—for the good of mankind, than to point out how much someone has been able to hoard and take from others and keep for their own use.

"There is even a television program that shows how the wealthy have squandered and wasted their wealth in their own self-gratification and in showing others how much they have. How sad! How much better it would be to show how they have utilized this gift for the good of all. Strangely enough, it will prove much more difficult to use such a gift wisely in helping others than it was to earn it in the first place.

"Further, how difficult, once the way has been found, to not boast about it but instead to help others also learn how it can be done. Their reward is the greatest gift of all— the knowledge that they are living as God meant them to live, not by the number of awards they win or the articles written on their generosity.

"One often hears nowadays about the goal of the young being to make money. For what use? Surely we can teach them better than that! We can teach them that money is the result of having a useful profession or capability, NOT the goal; that success is not measured by the amount of money or things we accumulate or spend; that we are all part of mankind and what happens to some of us happens to all of us; that we are born here on Earth for the purpose of growth, and learning, and helping others!"

Statement on The use of Time:

"How sad it is that we spend so much of our leisure or extra time in play, or just doing nothing. How wonderful and productive it would be if we allocated a portion of this very special gift of time in finding ways to help others. We must not just give a sum to an organization or church for the help of others and thus feel as though we have done our part, absolving ourselves of personally helping others. We must do it ourselves to develop ourselves. Don't ask, 'How can I help?' Rather look for problems and then try to help in their solution.

"Giving an expensive gift to someone is a waste of resources—both of yours when it could be used better to help others—and in the waste of effort and materials to make that gift in the first place. Better to tell them of the using of your time (the most valuable gift of all) to help others and doing so in their name.

"The proof of the true worth of someone is in their deeds and the amount of good they have done—not in their words or the wealth they have accumulated.

"One of the ex-presidents of the United States has spent much of his time since leaving office contributing his time to actually helping others building low-cost homes and other similar projects. How many do you know who are willing to make such an effort at that time in their life? Who are willing to give, not take?"

Statement on Learning:

"The television channels are currently filled with sex and violence and hate and the breaking of laws, and showing to all—especially the young—how self-indulgence and self-gratification pays off. Can the stations showing this honestly believe that this is not harmful to the society as well as to the individual? Some so-called studies are supposed to show that they are not harmful. What nonsense. How can studies today predict effects in the near and far distant future?

"How much better to show the good side of mankind instead of the bad. To teach how to help instead of how to hurt. How to get along in the world with the laws instead of how to break them. How to change laws if they are no longer applicable or are wrong, instead of how to get around or ignore them."

The following statement came from "Mother Earth" or "Pacha Mama" as I was writing this section:

"I, as Pacha Mama, accuse all those religions who are

opposed to abortion, of rape (of me)! This Earth that I am can no longer support any more children and it is essential that this continuing increase in production of beings be not only stopped, but significantly reduced, so that the total world population decreases. The religions who decry abortion are thinking only of themselves, not of my ability to provide resources to support them. Those religions don't have to support these beings. I do. My resources are badly over extended right now and we are already heading for disaster because of it. We are no longer in the Middle Ages when more devotees meant more wealth and more power to the religion who had them!

"To feed this continuing increase you are developing more productive food plants which require more fertilizer and more pesticides, and often more water. But I am still expected to provide the fertile earth and water and air to permit this greater production to occur. Your poisons and synthetics continue to destroy my attempts to balance this Earth in a myriad of ways, many of which you aren't even aware of.

"I must tell you to stop. Stop your increased production of humans. Stop your production of pesticides. Stop your production of synthetic fertilizers. Stop burning down my forests. Stop destroying my atmosphere. Stop trying to force me to give you greater production. Begin to realize that we are all one! When you harm me you harm yourself! When you try to make me do more than I am capable of, you reduce your ability to grow spirituality, which is all of our goals! Learn to work with me, and become one with me, and together we will do things undreamed of by you.

"Now, begin to prepare to reap what you have wrought for you have very little time to do so."
PACHA MAMA

October 10, 1991, 7 PM.

Question: On November 10, 1988 you said that I had been "One" with someone and lived in Atlantis. Please tell me about Atlantis. Where, when, etc.

"Atlantis was a continent in the middle area of the Atlantic Ocean. There is little or no trace of it today, even on the ocean floor, because it was so utterly destroyed by the combined actions of flood, tidal wave, earth quake and tectonic plate movement. Essentially nothing remains to indicate its presence. At the time of its existence—more than 10,000 years ago—it was a very advanced civilization and attempted to build what no one had ever done before—a true democracy. It didn't work because of human desires for power, and had to be destroyed so that a new and better start could be made. There were enough survivors scattered throughout the world to begin over without contamination of what had happened there.

"Unfortunately, the next attempt, primarily in the Tigris and Euphrates valleys, from about 4000 BC to about 10,000 BC, also failed for the same reason. This somewhat more advanced civilization (advanced in only some areas, but much less spiritual) also had to be destroyed in pretty much the same way as Atlantis."

(HK Note: Sir Leonard Woolley in his book Ur of the Chaldees described his belief that he discovered evidence of the Great Flood, dated at between 3500 and 4000 BC. in his diggings at Ur. Sir Max Mallowan more recently came to the conclusion that the Deluge in Babylonia, described in the Epic of the Flood, was a genuine historical event (which occurred in very remote Sumerian history), traces of which have been discovered in the excavations of Tell Fara (ancient Shuruppak) and perhaps at Kish, but not at Ur.)

"We now come to the present civilization starting at

about 4000 BC. Unfortunately, while advancing in some areas far more than either of the previous two civilizations—for instance in science—it has now reached the critical point where it has become obvious that, without a fresh start, and another step up in spiritual development, mankind's inhumanity to man and to other lifeforms cannot be sufficiently corrected to permit its further growth.

"Accordingly, forces utilized previously will be brought to bear again to sufficiently disrupt this civilization to permit a new start on the upward spiral toward eventual oneness with God.

"Times will be difficult for awhile, as new concepts and ideas are rushed to completion and old ideas are thrown out or reworked. However, the effort will be worth it, and a stunning new civilization will develop which will make the effort by all worthwhile. Remember, no one will be permanently lost. Each one lost at the present time will be brought back as their unique abilities and contributions can be utilized to help build the new and much softer and more gentle civilization.

"This new civilization will be a shinning example of mankind's ability to look after, and help, each other and all of nature—not just being concerned about himself or herself as we are today. With this attitude, all can grow mentally and spiritually although, as in the past, we each will continue to be individuals with our own unique past, abilities, and characteristics."

October 11, 1991, 2 PM.

Question: Is the Earth alone in the universe with Earth type people or are there others with similar physical characteristics?

"There are many other Earth type civilizations, both in our galaxy, and in other galaxies. There are also many other civilizations with dramatically different characteristics, such as the one you (HK) came from in which all are units of Light and Energy as opposed to having physical structures which may or may not include two arms, two legs, etc. Even in our present solar system there are other lifeforms, although you are not aware of them because you are looking for similarities to Earth type existence rather than energy forms and crystals which also contain life energies. Thus you have not yet developed sensors capable of detecting such dramatically different lifeforms.

"All the Universe is brimming over with life energies of thousands or millions of types. Each is struggling to learn and grow into oneness with God (Theirs) and finally GOD. In most cases there is little contact between different lifeforms because of the same lack of understanding of Life which you have. Occasionally, one will reach the point where it believes that it must try to contact other lifeforms and various types of missions will be sent out to look for it. Strangely enough, as with you, there are other intelligent lifeforms on their very planet which they are also unaware of, and which they could find, and learn from, much more easily than through interstellar travel. However, all are entitled to try for themselves to find whatever lifeforms they wish to look for.

"Some lifeforms that you might find in space, you will wish that you hadn't tried so hard to find because they may be very destructive to your present lifeforms or planet. Others will learn more from you than you from them. Some will be so far advanced from you that there will be little that can be learned by either.

"In general, finding and communicating with other lifeforms, that are similar enough to you to make it worthwhile, will not have been worth the effort, especially when there is so much more so close by (that is, on your very planet!) and with such a wealth of information to exchange with you.

"From this very brief discussion of space and some of its inhabitants, we hope you will begin to adjust your sights inward rather than outward, and begin to learn what is necessary for you to learn. That is, that we are all one, in a myriad of shapes, sizes, and capabilities and there is much, much more here on Earth for you to learn about, and, in fact, that you must learn about, and work with and for, if you are ever to succeed in reaching your magnitude."

Question: You say that great destruction will reign onto the Earth in the near future. What should we do and what should we not do to try to minimize this effect?

"First, let's look at what we should not do. There will be little point in trying to save the lives of vast numbers of people. A major part of the problem is that you have permitted far too many people to be on the Earth at one time. The Earth simply cannot provide the sustenance (food, water, air, and other necessities that you are not yet aware of) to adequately nurture this quantity of people at one time. You should not start storing vast quantities of food in selected spaces because many of these will be destroyed. Realize that most or all forms of transportable energy will no longer be available so don't expect business as usual. Don't collect guns so you can fight off mobs. There won't be many except, perhaps for a very short time in large cities.

"Now, what should you do? Begin immediately thinking of the Earth as a living being and treat it as such! It is alive, and VERY intelligent! Stop destroying its surface—that is, its plant and animal life and its soil. Stop spreading synthetic chemicals of all types on its surface. Stop trying to force it to produce far more than it is capable of. Stop covering its surface with concrete and asphalt. Stop dumping waste into its streams, rivers, lakes and oceans. You know not what you do! Don't wait ten years to clean up airborne pollution. Begin cleaning it up NOW—and as fast as you possibly can!

"Know that major weather changes are in store and be prepared to shift crops from one area of the world to another. Help each country and/or state to become as self-sufficient as possible. Help each individual family to become as self-sufficient as possible. Begin shifting your political process and funds from the federal to the state and then more and more to local levels. Become more and more a vegetarian as supplies of meat, fish, and fowl begin to disappear. Help your body to begin adjusting to this new diet as quickly as possible by having more and more meatless days.

"But most important of all, begin to treat each other more gently. Your, and their, lives may depend on it. Start realizing that we are all truly one and when you harm another (whether human or other lifeform) you harm yourself and the Earth you depend on for life and growth. Stop the present thinking process that what is good for me must also be good for others, and begin to truly cooperate and work together for the good of all!"

CHAPTER 14

FINAL COMMENTS
FROM THE SPIRITUAL HIERARCHY

Received November 22, 1991, 9AM

"This completes our first book on the past, present and future of the Earth. It is intended to teach Earthlings of their past and future so they will be able to more closely interact with Pacha Mama and make a more harmonious whole, helping all to grow together towards their magnitude.

"The words spoken here are as close to correct as we can make them in translating thought pictures and ideas into written words.

"It is hoped that the reader, and all those who are exposed to this wisdom and knowledge, will make as full use of it as they possibly can. It will help not only the individual, but also the whole race, to surmount the difficulties which are about to be inflicted on you because of your past and present transgressions.

"These words tell of a whole new way of life for you. It will be a life which will eventually develop into your becoming Gods. And yet, this will not occur without great difficulties and problems that you can't even imagine. Surmount these difficulties and solve these problems and you will find a way of life that is beyond your wildest dreams. But you will have to believe that it is possible and worth the stupendous effort required.

"Allow the energies described here to flow over and around and through you. These energies will then become a part of you and help you to carry out your individual and collective tasks and permit you to begin to know what wonders there are for you in the future.

"Be not concerned of the many deaths which are about to occur. None are lost but will simply be continuing their growth elsewhere until they will be needed again here. Remember that this transition is for your growth and its severity depends on your ability to learn and understand from what is given you in this book.

"We wish you well and are training guides to help you over this Great Transition. Listen to what they have to say, and if it sounds reasonable and practical to you, then try to carry out their suggestions. Even though you may not fully understand what they are telling you, it will be with your best interests in mind.

"We will continue to be in touch with you through our representatives there and, through each of you, as you develop the abilities described in this book of channeling us.

"Please remember that we are a part of you, and have spent eons of time trying to develop the full potential in you—often with you fighting us every step of the way. It has been difficult for both of us. And difficulties will continue until the final end when we all become one.

"Go with God"

If you would like additional copies of this book, see your local bookstore or use the order form provided below. (Please photocopy the form rather than tearing it out of this book.)

Please send_____ copies of
The Pure, Golden Light of Love to:

_____

_____

_____

_____

I enclose $18.00 US for each book. (Includes $2.00 shipping and handling within the continental US.) Overseas orders please add $2.00 more per book for a total of $20.00 US for each book. Canadian readers please send $22.00 Canadian per book including shipping.

Mail your order to :
SPIRIT HOUSE PRESS
P.O. Box 37163
Tucson, Arizona USA 85740-7163

About the author

H. King was born and raised in Alaska. He received a degree in chemical engineering in 1949 and immediately began a career in materials research and development. In 1955 he joined a major aerospace company so he could help pioneer in this new and exciting field, becoming what is now called a "rocket scientist". He continued working in this area as a director of research and technical director until his retirement in 1990. During this time he presented 24 technical papers in several related fields, received 5 patents, and was a featured speaker on a PBS TV program and a guest lecturer at many universities and technical conferences.

In 1968, while continuing his work in materials research, the author began a 25 year period investigating and trying to understand many of the great mysteries of mankind as well as endeavoring to learn more about the capabilities of the mind. This work included intensive study, meditation, and travel to most of the sacred places on Earth. In 1990 he moved from 16 forested acres in New Hampshire to a uniquely designed and located home in Arizona—where this book was written—to continue his studies.